Principal's Passion

Principal's Passion

A Quest for Quality Public Education

Susan A. Colton

My Castle Press, LLC

Copyright © 2018 by Susan A. Colton

All rights reserved, including the right to reproduce this book, or portions thereof, in any form. No part of this book may be used or reproduced in any manner whatsoever without written permission from the author, except in the case of brief quotations embodied in critical articles and reviews. The views expressed herein are the responsibility of the author and do not necessarily represent the position of the publisher. For information or permission, write: scolton@bellsouth.net.

This is a work of creative nonfiction. The events herein are portrayed to the best of the author's memory. While all the stories in this book are true, some names and identifying details may have been changed to protect the privacy of the people involved.

Editorial work and production management by Eschler Editing.
Cover design by Kimberly Kay Durtschi.
Interior print design and layout by Kimberly Kay Durtschi.
eBook design and layout by Joy Dawn Johnson.

Published by My Castle Press, LLC

First Edition: April 2018
Printed in the United States of America

10 9 8 7 6 5 4 3 2

ISBN 978-0-9997778-0-0 (softcover)
ISBN 978-0-9997778-1-7 (ebook)

To Chuck, my soulmate and the love of my life. Thank you for loving me for who I am and for being my biggest cheerleader throughout our thirty-two years together.

To my mom, Jeanne, my best friend and biggest advocate. Thank you for making me the kind, compassionate, independent woman I am today.

To my dad, Emmett, my first model toastmaster. You've been gone so long you never had a chance to see me become a principal, but you've been there on my shoulder as my guardian angel ever since.

To my special friend, Judy, who was always there with the biggest smile as a fellow teacher, traveler, shopper, and lifelong lover of books.

Acknowledgments

To all the students and families I have had the honor of serving over my thirty-plus years in education, I want to thank you for THE reason I was excited to get up and go to "work" each day. It was amazing to get to know all of you and provide you with a motivational school environment you could grow and thrive in. I hope I helped you believe in yourselves and taught you to reach for your dreams. I gave you my very best and always wanted to do more than humanly possible to provide you with a quality public education.

To all the teachers and staff I have had the pleasure and privilege of working with over the years, YOU are my heroes! You made us look good every day with your tireless, selfless work for the children. You taught me so much of what I know about the value of open, honest conversation and building positive, respectful, trustworthy relationships. I am in awe of your knowledge and skill at knowing precisely what each student needed and how to guide them to learning even above and beyond our lofty expectations. Your creative and innovative design of student work made me proud to say I was your colleague and partner in authentic learning. I salute you!

For my family, who was always my biggest cheerleader and endured my early mornings, late nights, busy weekends, and my 24/7 commitment to my schools—I love and appreciate you! To my dad, my mom, and my husband and soulmate, I have dedicated this book to your memory. To my brother, sister-in-law, and three beautiful nieces, you have helped me through my toughest times with your demonstration of love, patience, support, and understanding, as well as your precious gifts of journals and pens, glittery travel cups, and a coffee mug that says "Get It Done!"

To my esteemed friends and colleagues, my teachers, mentors, and role models, I thank you for believing in me, encouraging me, and joining me in my exciting educational and life journey. I have always wanted to be there for you and exceed your expectations, not for me but to make all of you proud. To the late Dr. Phillip Schlechty and the late Marilyn Hohmann, your visionary leadership and lessons on transforming schools changed my life. Dr. Verda Farrow, I am forever grateful for the opportunity to begin my career as your assistant principal and to learn from your exemplary qualities as a servant-leader. To Carole Michel, my administrative assistant and confidant, for being by my side from the day I became a principal and throughout every detail involved in realizing the dream of opening our new school.

For my new Quantum Leap family of authors, marketers, coaches, and fellow leapers—almost a year has passed since we first met in March 2017. It was at that first meeting in Philadelphia that I put pen to paper and wrote my big, hairy, audacious goal of writing and publishing my first book within a year! And here we are. I especially thank Ann McIndoo and Misheal Patton for their role in helping me get the book out of my head, and Geoffrey Berwind for helping me get my stories on paper. Thank you to the amazing Martha Bullen, Tamara Richardt, Raia King, and Brian Edmondson for their roles in getting my content organized, my marketing plan made, and my publicity materials and website created. But "Most Important," thank you, Steve Harrison, for moving me forward out of my comfort zone to make my connection commitments.

Finally, I would like to thank my editor, Heidi Brockbank with Eschler Editing, for pushing and challenging my thought process, Michele Preisendorf for her excellent copyedit, and for Kimberly Durtschi, my book designer, who made my vision a reality! Special thanks to my influencers, THE Peter Yarrow, who inspires millions of educators with his music, "Don't Laugh at Me," and his commitment to making schools "bully-free zones," and George Thompson for providing the practical proof that "Working on the Work" really works and for continuing the Schlechty Center legacy. Also, thanks to Carlie Craig, an extremely positive, talented, and engaged student who was destined for fame and success and is now living her BIG dream in Hollywood, and to

Dr. Hirofumi Hamada, a friend and professor from Japan, for allowing me to be a part of his research and study of leadership in American public schools and systems.

Contents

Preface i

Introduction v

Chapter One:
From Chaos to Calm 1

Chapter Two: Common-Sense
Solutions and Problem-Solving 13

Chapter Three: What If Students
Topped the Organizational Chart? 21

Chapter Four: The Theme Queen:
Using Metaphors for Educational Change 37

Chapter Five: Building Positive
Relationships in Diverse Communities 51

Chapter Six: Who's
Running the Schoolhouse? 59

Chapter Seven: Engaging
Communities in Public Education 69

Chapter Eight: Testing versus
Teaching: Killing the Joy of Learning 87

Chapter Nine: Public Education:
The Cornerstone of Our Democracy 97

Chapter Ten: How to Rally
Communities to Save Public Schools 105

The Dream Continues 115

References and Resources 117

Note to the Reader 123

About the Author 125

Preface

I'm passionate about public education and have had the privilege of positively influencing thousands of students, teachers, parents, and community members to create caring and motivating learning environments in public schools. I've done this by actively engaging everyone in a process of building relationships that support students and families on the path to achieving success.

On Friday, March 27, 1992, I was attending a workshop at my school system's TV studio, learning how to produce a video to market our school. It was a teacher's planning day, and I was an assistant principal at the elementary school I had been assigned to just before Thanksgiving 1987. I was an aspiring principal yet had been told in the past by my best of friends that I would never be a principal because I was "too nice."

That morning I received a call from my supervising principal to meet her bosses, the area superintendent and area director, at an Italian restaurant close to the school at noon. They were going to take me to lunch and then to another nearby elementary school where they had just "removed" the current principal and cleaned out her office. I would be appointed "acting principal" of that school. I immediately left the workshop and drove the twenty miles to the restaurant. My heart was pounding in my throat, and my thoughts were racing at the prospect of finally becoming a principal, meeting the teachers and staff, and dealing with the current chaos at that school. I met these two prominent and respected women leaders for lunch and was given an overview of my new position. The parents at this school were meeting at clandestine locations to plot against the teachers and the principal, and the teachers, I was told, were wearing black armbands in protest of the parents and the principal and what they were being asked to do.

To this day, I cannot remember what I ate for lunch, but I do remember that I was basically told my job would be to "heal" and bring order to this school in chaos. I was also told by the area director to go home and change from the pantsuit I was wearing into a suit with a skirt so that I would be presented properly as the new "acting principal." At 2:00 p.m., I faced my new school staff and was introduced as someone who would listen to their needs and do the right thing for the children. They were also warned by the area superintendent that their previous behavior was unacceptable and that each of them needed to step up to eliminate the cancerous environment spreading through their school.

When I finally got to speak, the words coming from my heart, I told them I knew we had a lot of work to do but I would be there, right beside them, doing what was right for the children. I told them I would listen to their concerns and work with them to address those concerns and find solutions that were reasonable and acceptable. I made eye contact with each one of them, pausing briefly as I did so, hoping they would feel valued and recognized. I also told them we would set a date to meet with the parents to hear their concerns in an organized manner. After I spoke, several teachers came up to say "Welcome" and that they were looking forward to working with me. I felt these teachers were sincerely willing to work with me to resolve the existing conflicts so they could get back to the business of teaching and learning.

For the remainder of that school year, I made sure I did three things every day:

- Listen, listen, listen
- Do what you say, and say what you do
- Value each person as an individual

In addition, of course, I hired an assistant principal, promoted a highly regarded person on the office staff to be my office manager/confidential secretary, and met with each teacher and staff member to hear their concerns. Within the first week we also met as a staff with the parents in our school cafeteria. It was standing room only. We set ground rules and time limits for speaking, and other than a couple of shouting matches and discovering a parent taping the whole thing with a tape recorder stashed in her purse, we all managed to get out alive! By the end of the school year, our staff had established ourselves as a "Shared-Decision-Making School" through the district teachers' union and scheduled a series of team-building activities, including a ropes course. Our School Advisory Council, which was made up of parents, teachers, and community members, met on a regular basis and began to plan for the following school year, answering questions and concerns in specific detail along the way. By July 1, I was officially appointed principal.

As you can imagine, I was physically drained by this chaotic experience, but I was able to bring order to my new 24/7 world and was emotionally supercharged by the possibilities that raced through my head day and night. Financially, with the title of principal came the principal's salary schedule, and I felt like I had earned the opportunity to finally make the appropriate salary. Spiritually I prayed a lot—for strength, for persistence, and for the courage I would need to lead this school community and its students to the amazing outcomes I envisioned for our future.

I pulled from each of my leadership resources as I planned for the opening of my first full school year as a principal. *The 7 Habits of Highly Effective People* by Stephen R. Covey helped frame my thinking for the tone I wanted set for our work in the coming year. I had just completed a leadership course on the seven habits and had the opportunity to see Dr. Covey in person in a nearby city over the summer. I was inspired, I was energized, and I was excited to "sharpen my saw" as I became fully engaged in the continuous, quality improvement of my school.

The following year, I attended a Disney Institute "Creating Motivational Learning Environments" seminar, and by 1995 I was selected by my superintendent to be one of forty principal leaders to be trained as a facilitator for a statewide leadership initiative. This Institute for Florida School Principals would train principals from all sixty-seven school districts across the state through the Florida Department of Education and the Florida Association of School Superintendents' Academy for School

Executives. Nationally recognized leader of school reform Dr. Phillip Schlechty was to present "Leading Schools to Quality Results" and the "Working on the Work" framework as the content. Little did I know the profound effect this opportunity would have on my life as a principal. It changed my work in ways that even I couldn't imagine!

Fast-forward to 1999–2000, when I would receive two awards: the Florida State Commissioner's Principal Award for Outstanding Leadership and the National Distinguished Principal Award by the U.S. Department of Education and the National Association of Elementary School Principals. These awards reflected the eight years of outstanding work and leadership my students, teachers, staff, and parents and community members contributed to our school. I accepted both awards on their behalf. My district also rewarded my hard work with my appointment as principal of a new school being built and allowed me the privilege of opening it as an "entrepreneurial school" I could create and design.

Fast-forward to now. I am a retired principal still living and volunteering in my school district. For the past three years I have served as a caretaker for my mother, who passed away in February, and for my husband, who also passed away this last December. I am in the process of reinventing myself and discovering who I am at this point in my life.

I am writing this book to share my experiences and my success in being able to influence thousands of students, teachers, parents, and community members to become partners in the educational process of their children. I want to show you that building positive relationships in diverse communities and putting students at the "top of the organizational chart" really works. I also would like to share what I learned about using themes as metaphors for creating motivational learning environments and engaging everyone in the process of change. And I want to create a sense of urgency for schools and their communities to rally together to "save" public schools from corporate charter takeover and help make public schools a priority again! I believe we can bring back the professionalism of teachers and educators and restore the trust in allowing those with the expertise and experience to make decisions that matter for our public schools.

I believe there is hope . . .

Introduction

Will We Let the End of Public Education be the End of Our Democracy?

Are you an educator who is tired of teaching to the test, whose creativity and innovation have been dismissed by arbitrary evaluation systems, and who would like to be respected and rewarded as the professional you've spent your lifetime to be?

Are you a parent who wants your child to be excited about going to school every day instead of having test anxiety; who wants to see their child grow and develop intellectually, socially, and emotionally; and who would like to be more involved in your neighborhood school, but you don't know exactly where to begin?

Are you a small business or professional with expertise in your field and a wealth of real-world experience to offer students, teachers, and families, who would like to lend your talents and services to your local schools and partner with them to prepare the next generation of citizens and workers?

If you answered yes to any of the questions above, then fasten your seat belt, and answer the call to action in *Principal's Passion: A Quest for Quality Public Education*. After twenty-two years as an elementary-school principal and over thirty years in education, I want to share the successful experiences I've had with thousands of students, teachers, parents, and community members in becoming partners in the educational process of our children. I believe our children are the future of our democracy and of our humanity, of our country and of our world.

In the first half of this book, I will do just that—share my stories, my learning, and the methods and processes that worked for me. But in no way have I done this alone, without the wisdom and guidance of mentors, without the dedication and trust of teachers and colleagues, or with a magic formula I invented myself. Because this is not about me; it is about all the people who came together on my journey to educate and serve our children, their families, and our community at large. It is about using common-sense solutions and proven problem-solving methods. It is about a collaborative culture of caring in schools that puts children first. It is also about creating innovative, motivational learning environments that authentically engage all students.

We've all heard the African proverb "It takes a village to raise a child." In fact, when I grew up, everyone in my town knew everyone else and made sure all children were where they were supposed to be and doing what they were supposed to do. If you grew up in a neighborhood like that, you can probably remember your mom knowing exactly where you had been between your walk from school to home. Today, our villages are larger and our world is global and more diverse, but I believe we can build a sense of community for our children and ourselves. We must value our humanity and celebrate our diversity as we come together to create a safe school environment where everyone has a voice.

In the second half of this book, I discuss the uncertain future of public schools and what has happened to education in the last several decades—how education has become big business, with more corporations profiting from the educational policies they lobby for and which are passed by politicians. I will also talk about how the focus of public education in the media has been the failure of the system, the schools, the teachers, and the students, how they all must be held accountable with increasingly more evaluations and tests, and how they cannot be trusted.

What happened to the joy of learning, the debate, the laughter, and the fun of children exploring new ideas and knowledge by trying over and over until they figure it out and get it right? It seems there is no time these days for conversation about learning and the sharing of different points of view. What happened to "Listen to your teacher" presented in a positive way to children by supportive parents? What happened to the connection between the home and the village shopkeepers to keep our children safe? Schools can rebuild these bridges between the home, the school, and the community. We can teach our families how to become involved with the schools and welcome our businesses in helping us prepare our students for the workplace.

The history of public education shows our country's intent to create a knowledgeable electorate and equality in opportunity for all. The American Dream and the cornerstone of our democratic process was our forefathers' vision for a free and appropriate education for all. Now our democracy hangs in the balance of public schools versus privatization by for-profit corporations whose vision is to pad their pockets on the backs of our country's children, and not to serve the common good. We must engage our communities to support public schools by inviting everyone—including our local, state, and national government officials—in to see the incredible work our students and teachers are doing every day. We must market our schools and create positive publicity to bring back public trust.

I believe in the power of relationships and in all of us—students, teachers, parents, and community members—working together as partners to save our public schools from corporate takeover. I will show you how to do it, who needs to be involved, and how to do it without spending any additional taxpayer dollars. Do you think we can create a movement? Will you make a commitment to be involved? I have hope that the collective power of the human spirit can connect one community at a time, and together across our great country, we can change the future of public education. Our future depends on it!

From Chaos to Calm

My passionate purpose for writing this book is twofold. First, I want to share with you my past experiences in creating successful innovative and motivational learning environments in public schools. Second, I want to give you an insider viewpoint on what's happening with public schools today, persuade you to rally your communities to save our public schools from privatization, and bring back the joy of learning. I would like to begin by going back to my story and the reason I do what I do from the preface and give you more detail on how I brought my first school out of chaos and back to an orderly environment where teaching and learning and the students were the top priority.

Imagine you are an assistant principal aspiring to be a principal, and one day when you least expect it, you are being summoned to heal the divisions of a school in chaos and get everyone back to the task of teaching and learning. In March of 1992, that happened to me. It was a teachers' planning day, and I was attending a workshop at our school district's television studio, learning how to make a video to market our school. I received a phone call from my supervising principal to meet with the area superintendent and area director at an Italian restaurant close to the school at noon. I was told the current principal had been removed, the parents were meeting in clandestine locations to plot against the teachers and principal, the teachers were wearing black armbands in protest, and I would be appointed acting principal. To this day, I cannot remember what I ate for lunch, but I do remember being told to go home and change my pantsuit for a suit with a skirt before I met my school staff. I also remember my heart pounding in my throat and my thoughts racing at the prospect of meeting the teachers and taking charge of the current chaos at the school.

At 2:00 p.m. I greeted the teachers and staff and spoke from my heart. I told them I knew we had a lot of work to do but that I would be there, working right beside them, to do what was right for the children. I also told them I would listen to their concerns and work with them to find solutions that were reasonable and acceptable. I paused and made eye contact with each person, hoping they would sense that I was sincere and that they would feel valued and recognized.

For the rest of this school year and beyond, I made sure I did these three things every day:

1) Listen, Listen, Listen

In Stephen R. Covey's *The Seven Habits of Highly Effective People*, habit five is "Seek First to Understand, Then to Be Understood."

I was fortunate I had recently completed a leadership course on the Seven Habits of Highly Effective People and had even had the opportunity of meeting Dr. Covey in person at a seminar in a nearby city. My work with the Covey Institute was instrumental in framing my thinking about listening to others, understanding where they were coming from, and not imposing my ideas or solutions on anyone until I was crystal clear on their position. I was anxious to put my learning into practice and affirm what I believed was right. Here are some tips on the things I used when listening to others:

- **Listening to understand others** and their viewpoints and concerns is most important when coming into an unfamiliar environment with a group of people you are charged with leading. Be sure to ask clarifying questions for deeper understanding, such as "I'm not quite sure what you mean by . . ." or "Could you tell me more about . . . ?" or "I thought I heard you say . . . Is that correct?" Asking the right questions helps others feel like you are clarifying any confusion you may have about what they are saying. Taking brief notes on burning issues that arise with each person will also help you remember what is most important in resolving their individual concerns and reassure them that you are serious about hearing their personal point of view. Make sure you respond to their ideas by nodding your head or with a brief verbal acknowledgment, but do not offer an immediate commitment to their idea or resolution until you have heard from everyone and have had time to reflect on the big picture.

- **Listening with empathy** is identifying deeply and emotionally with another person and connecting with their feelings without judgment. Listen to their words, but also listen to the emotion in their voice, the look in their eye, and their total body language to learn as much as you can. Do not be tempted to relate a similar story you may have experienced; just focus on them and where they are coming from so the conversation does not break down. Acknowledge that you hear what they are saying with "I think I heard you say . . ." to give further clarification and meaning to the emotion they are sharing with you. Whatever you do, do not say "I know exactly how you feel," because unless you've walked in their shoes, you don't!

- **Listening without interrupting and responding** takes practice and control but builds trust when communicating with someone who may not have the same beliefs or opinions you do. Take the time needed to hear each person out, even if it requires several meetings. You will be rewarded in the future by the amount of time you spend in the present, listening and understanding points of view, and you will build stronger relationships overall. Make notes of the opinions and beliefs that may not resonate with yours so that you can address those ideas later during the problem-solving process.

Being a good listener is the first step to building trust with an individual and eventually the total group. Remember what is important to each person and start each new conversation with something positive and meaningful to them. Be sure to call them by name and make eye contact in both formal meetings and informal meetings, such as in the hallway or lunchroom. Asking how things are going with a particular lesson or student or offering a smile and an encouraging word will make others feel comfortable with you and reinforce that you genuinely care about them and their well-being. Modeling the listening process for others repeatedly begins to catch on as you observe others in their interactions.

2) Do What You Say, and Say What You Do

Another way of building trust with others is to do what you say and say what you do. Showing others that you are sincere, consistent, and trustworthy takes time, but others will soon realize that you are a person of your word.

- **Do not make promises you know you cannot keep.** Making promises can be a reaction for a leader who wants to please or a strategy for a staff member who wants to catch you off guard while you are on the way to another situation and your mind is on something else. Be honest in your assessment of the situation or request. If you know it is against policy and procedure, say no, but offer to follow up later to review why you cannot grant the request. Do not try to be the good guy and just say anything to fix the problem! Instead, offer suggestions or possible alternatives without making a firm commitment until you have time to research the possibilities and consequences.

- **Follow through with what you tell others you are going to do next.** Be sure to give yourself a reasonable amount of time for your actions, such as the end of the week or the beginning of the following week. Follow up on your conversation with a note or email restating what you said you were going to do and the timeline, whether that involves an individual or an entire staff. If it is an individual, get back to that person with your results before presenting it to the whole group. If it is the group, allow time for discussion and questions.

- **Don't make it up!** If you don't know the answer, admit it, and say you'll get back to the person who asked. You do not know all the answers, but you do know who and where to get them from. Again, give yourself a reasonable timeline to research the information and to respond. When appropriate, you may ask the person to assist you in the research and involve them in the problem-solving process and solution.

- **Be consistent, matching your words with your actions**. "Walk your talk." Do not try to be the hero; be human. If you find you cannot do something you said you'd do because of a rule or law you cannot change, admit your mistake, apologize, and move on. If it is a serious situation and you've said that a repeat offense would result in a consequence, then follow through with the consequence. Meeting with a teacher and a union representative can be the best thing for everyone involved. Remember, "They do not care how much you know until they know how much you care."

Asking others for feedback on how things are going as often as possible is an excellent way to keep a finger on the pulse of your organization. Remember something that was important to an individual and ask them how it is coming along. Begin each group meeting with a "How are we doing with . . . ?" question. Don't be afraid to ask for fear of what the answer may be. Being genuinely open to others' thoughts and opinions and spending time discussing differences will keep you on the road to continuous quality improvement.

3) Value Each Individual, Along with Their Values and Opinions

It is not enough just to believe that each individual is unique and brings value to your organization; you must act on that belief. Listening to their voice and what they value in life is a first step but continuing that conversation and showing them you believe they have value is key. These are some things I did to encourage open, honest communication in my groups:

- **You do not have to agree with everyone's opinion; you can always "agree to disagree."** A variety of opinions can lead to rich discussion and debate as you bring ideas forward to a larger group. Be sure to chart the different points of view so that everyone can see the pros and cons of each idea, and honor and value each opinion as it is presented and discussed. Opinion charts are valuable and can be used for any future shared decision-making sessions you hold.

- **Treat everyone with respect as you work to earn their respect.** When working with a larger group, listen carefully to the thoughts presented, and repeat what you heard each person say to their satisfaction before you commit it to the chart. Honor diverse ideas and diverse backgrounds and put everything on the discussion table without passing judgment. You should not consider any thought or idea too foolish or unworthy to post.

- **Set ground rules by consensus before you begin each discussion session.** Everyone should have the same amount of time to speak; no one should dominate the conversation. Ask others to listen with respect and put themselves in the speaker's shoes to try to understand where they are coming from as they present their ideas. You should also allow participants to ask clarifying questions for greater understanding.

- **Remember the Golden Rule: treat others the way you want them to treat you.** Be proactive, not reactive, and think before you speak or respond to others. Ask yourself, "How would I feel if this happened to me?" Maya Angelo once said, "I've learned that that people will forget what you said, people will forget what you did, but people will never forget how you made them feel."

- **Encourage out-of-the-box thinking; do not let the status quo limit the possibilities.** Asking a lot of what-ifs will cause others to stop and think beyond their normal boundaries. Nothing should be too outrageous for discussion—unless it is against the law! One technique that worked for me was using a film clip with teachers to illustrate something that might be considered "out of the box." I learned this technique at a Disney Institute course that focused on creating motivational learning environments within schools. An example was a film clip from Whoopi Goldberg and her 1992 movie, *Sister Act*, where she played Sister Mary Clarence, who took over a nun's choir. With her "rock-star" approach, they could pull people, both young and old, off the neighborhood streets and back into the church to fill the seats. Why? Because their songs were current, energetic, and touched others in a way that made them want to dance and sing, snap their fingers, clap their hands, and join in the spirit of community. My question: Could changes like this be made in schools to cause students to want to be in their seats every day?

Developing Human Capital

Human capital is the value each person brings to their organization or community. This value includes talents, skills, experience, knowledge, training, and judgment and can be measured both individually and collectively. Investing in human capital is essential to buy-in from your staff and the achievement of your school's goals.

- **Each person has something positive to offer the group or organization.** Meaningful professional development opportunities are one of the most effective ways to increase employee engagement. I have found that these opportunities are also a way to recognize and draw out those who do not always contribute to a conversation. The key here, though, is that the professional development must be meaningful to the individual and not forced by "the powers that be." Some of my criteria are: the focus must always be on the students and their ability to be successful, the teacher must come back and present what they learned to at least one other colleague, and they must ask for feedback during the sharing process without fear of negativity or embarrassment.

- **Find out what your employees' talents and expertise are, and give them a task that will make them shine!** Ask for volunteers to share their successes in trying something they learned at their training in their classrooms. Also ask for volunteers to share "lessons learned" for ideas they've tried that might not have been successful, reinforcing the culture that it is safe to take a risk here. Asking "What do you think you would do next time?" opens a conversation about what could be changed in the lesson to result in success and thinking about their students' ages and stages of learning.

- **Give positive feedback when you see behavior you are looking for, or "catch them doing good," as we would say with our students.** Compliment others every day on something specific you see or hear them doing or saying. Reinforce the behaviors you want to see by modeling them yourself and through recognition of another's accomplishments. Engage in a conversation with that person about how they feel regarding a change they have made and how it has improved their teaching or their students' learning.

- **Give constructive feedback for questionable actions and ask, "How could you have done that differently?"** Always allow the person time for reflection and to gather their thoughts about their actions. Be very clear as to what actions and behaviors you expect. Let the person know that you know they will handle it more appropriately the next time. The feedback should be constructive and not punitive in any way.

- **Turn each person's unique talent(s) into positive performance.** Marcus Buckingham, author and business-management consultant for the Gallup Organization, articulates this as "Focus on your strengths and manage your weaknesses." To do this it is essential that each person identify both their strengths and where they believe they need additional knowledge or help with a weakness. Allowing others to share their talents in small groups will help them feel safe and do much to build self-confidence. Build teams so there are members with a variety of talents who support others who are not talented in those same areas. A culture of teamwork and collaboration will grow and evolve with time well spent.

Allowing everyone to attend professional development opportunities they are excited about and which they believe will help them in their daily work will contribute to their personal, continuous quality improvement as well as that of the organization. Sending staff members in pairs or small groups encourages collaboration beyond the time in training, whether it be during the workshop lunch break, driving to and from the workshop in the car, or continuing the conversation and learning back at the school. Arranging time within the school day for others to share or observe someone else doing something they would like to learn more about builds professionalism and a positive climate for personal and collective learning and growth.

One of the most rewarding experiences of my twenty-two years as an elementary school principal was nurturing others as they grew and developed into all they could be!

Encouraging teacher assistants to complete their degrees and then hiring them as teachers and promoting exceptional teachers to positions where they would have a greater impact on students, teachers, and families was particularly gratifying. Watching a teacher grow and achieve as a leader and future assistant principal and then principal was a real testament to developing human capital.

Building Relationships

Building relationships on all levels is another essential skill to add to your toolbox. In our world of technology, it is common to feel isolated despite all the emails and texts we're constantly sending and receiving. Actual face-to-face communication is important as it allows the true meaning of your words to be heard and felt. This is true for both internal and external relationships.

My advice is "Don't send the email." Meeting with the individual or group is more personal and effective.

- **Relationships are a two-way street, but as the leader, you must reach out to others first.** Be positive and caring in your outreach, keeping an open mind and an open heart. Put yourself in the other person's shoes, doing your best to understand them as you begin to build a rapport. Sometimes this requires you to take a leap of faith and get out of your comfort zone.

- **Building relationships can be difficult but rewarding.** The time spent is well worth it in the future and will multiply your results. There is no time limit on how long it takes to get to know others and their intentions. Do not assume anything by interpreting body language or by listening to what you may have heard from others. Most people want to do an excellent job and just need clarity about your expectations.

- **Strong internal relationships are important as they present unity to the outside world.** As the saying goes, "A staff that plays together stays together!" Take time to relax and have fun! Providing support to your employees when dealing with outside forces is an absolute necessity. In the case of difficult interactions, ask your employee how they might have handled things differently *after* the parent leaves and not while they are present.

- **Do not ask another person to do something you would not do yourself.** Be reasonable in your expectations of others. You are not above those you lead; you are a team player, and there should never be a double standard. Grab a broom or mop and clean the floors! There is nothing more powerful than rolling up your sleeves and getting in the trenches.

- **Open and honest relationships lead to the creation of highly effective teams.** We should always be transparent in sharing information with others. The more correct information you share, the less likely it is that you will have to deal with the incorrect rumor mill that spreads like wildfire. *If* information is power, then you should *not* be the "Powerful *One*." Empower others by sharing information and educating them with open, honest communication.

"Trust is the glue of life. It is the most essential ingredient in effective communication. It's the foundational principle that holds all relationships."
—Dr. Stephen R. Covey

Common-Sense Solutions and Problem-Solving

After establishing some rapport and trust with the staff, it was time to make a plan of action and to implement that plan. As a staff, we decided on a shared decision-making approach to identify and solve problems, which reinforced the value of each individual and allowed everyone to have a voice in the process. Strategic grouping to form teams and scheduling time for those teams to work, plan, and play together added to our positive relationship building and trust.

During those first few months, one of the first ideas to come from the staff was participating with the local teachers' union in a new partnership as a Shared Decision-Making School. Teachers, staff, administration, and parents would be trained in a process that allowed all stakeholders to have a voice in the decisions made at the school level. We agreed as a unified group to move forward, and volunteers from each subgroup became representatives for teachers, staff, and parents. Both my assistant principal and I would take part as administrators so everyone would know that we, as "the administration," were onboard.

One of the first activities we were involved in was a trust-building exercise that included a low ropes course. This consisted of a series of obstacles designed to challenge teams to use their resources to work together to accomplish a task. It was set up by a qualified team in the grassy area behind the school and held on a Saturday, which was a recommendation from the teachers so that everyone could take part. It included balance beams, a "spider web," "trust fall" circles, and other games that were low-risk and managed by group members who assumed critical spotting roles. The results? We experienced some eye-opening emotions, such as the fear of failing and the fear of losing control, as well as emerging self-confidence, leadership, and relationship building.

Shared Decision-Making

Here are some essential rules to setting up a successful shared decision-making process:

- **Set ground rules for a process that allows everyone to be involved in major decisions that affect the majority.** Ground rules should always build on the spirit of cooperation and respect, allowing time for participants to read and understand expectations. Ask participants if they would like to contribute any additional ground rules to the list, and then ask for consensus rather than a vote. You should always post a list of the agreed-upon ground rules as a reminder at every shared decision-making meeting.

- **Give each person the opportunity for others to hear their voice.** Allow time for everyone to speak, and set limits for "airtime" so the same individuals do not dominate the conversation. Encourage the participation of those who do not speak by asking for others to contribute, but do not call them out or demand it. A good tip for drawing "nonparticipants" into the conversation is to ask a question about a topic you know they are passionate about.

- **Use consensus building to reach the results so there are no winners and losers.** Never take a "vote" on whether to include an item or statement. If there is disagreement, discuss both sides of the issue and ask for consensus again on any changes. Think win-win, and ask if both sides will agree to disagree and if they can "live with" the results.

- **Build a sense of school as community, where each person can depend on others.** You, as the leader, set the tone for the conversation so that everyone knows they are there for the same outcome. Using icebreakers to mix up the discussion groups will give a variety of members an opportunity to get to know and learn to trust one another. Your communication must always portray the fact that "we are in this together and are there to support one another."

- **We must hold ourselves and each other accountable to the process and the results.** Remember, shared decision-making is a process that takes time, so do not try to rush or force the process or results. As one of my former teachers used to say, "Trust the process," and I would have to add, "And take lots of deep, cleansing breaths!"

Collaboration and Cooperation

Collaboration and cooperation are sometimes used interchangeably, but, really, they have distinct definitions and goals. Think about some examples where you may have used cooperative learning groups with your students or collaborated with your peers to plan a lesson or unit. What was different?

- **Individuals must practice working together toward a common goal.** Working together is also a process that takes lots of practice. Cooperation means everyone is working toward the same outcome or product but each person has a separate task to carry out to piece the puzzle together and reach that goal. Collaboration is more difficult because everyone is working on the same task, so each person must trust the others and come together to agree on how the outcome or product will look. Even though these terms may be used interchangeably, cooperation is more about getting along, whereas collaboration is more about giving and taking until an agreeable solution is met.

- **Develop a common language for the work so everyone is on the same page.** Define the terms you are going to use, and ask questions to clarify any confusion. Practice using this common language when communicating formally or informally, in writing and in speaking, to describe your work. Make sure everyone has multiple copies of this list of terms and sees them posted in high-traffic areas.

- **Treat everyone fairly and equally.** Mutual respect is essential among teams in developing trust, so always model the behavior you expect to see in return. Everyone must have the opportunity to contribute to the group work, allowing natural leaders to emerge as opposed to leadership being forced. Each person must have a chance to play each role within the group and to practice role-playing scenarios and outcomes that could occur. Remember the "Gallup Rule" of focusing on strengths and managing weaknesses.

- **Facilitate the development of relationships to make connections within and between the teams.** You, as the leader, must be the facilitator of relationship building. Group people together so they complement each other and draw on each other's strengths. Next, mix up the groups so there is a diversity of both knowledge and thought that stimulates rich debate and conversation. Again, allow enough time for each of these scenarios to occur and reoccur through practice, practice, practice, so that the process becomes second nature.

Problem-Solving

Just as in solving a word problem in mathematics, there are certain steps that must be followed in reaching an acceptable solution. I have found these next steps to be successful:

- **Identify the problem and define it** by asking the following questions: "Who does the problem affect?" "What does the problem look like?" and "How would things look without the problem?" Then identify the goals you want to achieve by eliminating the problem or changing something causing the problem, and determine how eliminating or changing the problem would affect other issues.

- **Identify the barriers to achieving your goals.** Is there a lack of funding or resources, a lack of support for change, or is there a law or policy that would prohibit you implementing your goal? Next, brainstorm potential solutions, discuss them, and gather data to support your thinking. For each potential solution, list the pros and cons, and research and present data to support the recommended solution. Finally, ask if the solution is long-term or a "quick fix."

- **Decide on a solution and a course of action, and continue to monitor the results for success.** How will you present the action plan in a unified manner to the community? Who will assume responsibility for each step of the action plan, and what is your timeline? How will you measure success, and who will record the data? Each of these actions is an essential step toward a successful solution. Monitoring progress must be ongoing, and results must be evaluated along the way. The action plan may be modified if needed, and regular, focused follow-up is critical to the entire process.

Common-Sense Solutions

Common-sense solutions are ones that are clear, practical, and made by sound judgment. They must benefit the common good of the people affected by the decided-upon actions and results. For example:

- **Make sure the solutions you choose are feasible for the parties you choose to carry them out.** Do the identified parties need more knowledge or training? Can this knowledge or training occur internally, or is outside help needed? Are the identified parties willing to participate for the long haul?

- **Do the solutions you choose rely on additional resources that are not available**, such as budgetary restrictions, if you identify specific dollars? Are there people willing and able to provide the knowledge or training needed, and if more work is required, how will it be compensated?
- **The solutions must be fair and equitable to all parties involved.** Look closely at each group affected by the changes you agree to make, and determine whether the solutions will put any undue pressure or stress on anyone. Is there consensus that something that currently exists must be eliminated?
- **Be sure to ask essential questions like** "Would I like this for *my* children?" Put yourself in others' shoes, and see if the solution fits for each child and family. Simplify the process as much as possible, and be clear with the explanation for the change. Everyone should ask themselves, "Can I live with this?"
- **Remember, Voltaire once said, "Common-sense is not so common!"**

Teamwork

"Two heads are better than one" and "Many hands make light work" are two expressions that come to mind when I think of teamwork. Working together as a team to solve problems and accomplish goals is much more effective than one or two people making all the decisions. It is also valuable in allowing each team member to share their strengths while learning to trust and rely on each other and sharing accountability for the solutions. Building effective teams requires you as a leader to provide the time and opportunity for individuals to work together.

- **Schedule time for team-building activities which will develop trust and camaraderie.** Begin each meeting with an icebreaker so everyone gets to know each other outside their work roles. Team problem-solving activities foster creativity, the sharing of ideas, and provide opportunities to support one another. Teams should reflect diversity of culture, personality, and ideas so that a difference in opinions and backgrounds will bring new perspectives to old ways of thinking and doing.

- **Allow time for individual teams to work, plan, and play together**. Building time into a traditional workday for common planning time will contribute to a positive climate in the workplace. "Breaking bread," or having lunch together, is another way to break down barriers and offer teams a more relaxing experience. I also found that taking everyone off campus to a different venue stimulates conversation and new learning and adds overall value and professionalism for participants.

- **Dr. Ken Blanchard, author of *High Five! The Magic of Working Together*, reminds us that "none of us is as smart as all of us."** He illustrates his point by showing how, if we are all in the same boat, we cannot be rowing in different directions. To create synergistic relationships where we are interdependent on one another and our strengths, we must work (or row) together toward the same vision, goals, and outcomes to be successful. I have used Dr. Blanchard's inspirational books throughout my career to show how leadership capacity can be built within an organization.

Relationships

When people use each other's strengths and talents within a team, the collective knowledge and expertise grows exponentially. Team members will continue to build greater trust with each other as they see positive results. The creation of a safe, risk-free environment without fear of retaliation or consequences encourages innovative ideas to grow and thrive in classrooms for the ultimate benefit of the students.

> *"We can improve our relationships by leaps and bounds if we become encouragers instead of critics."*
> —Joyce Meyer

What If Students Topped the Organizational Chart?

When you think of an organizational chart for schools or school systems, who is at the top?

Who is at the bottom of the chart, and how many layers of bureaucracy are in between? Normally, the superintendent or principal tops the organizational chart, but in reality, the state and national government decision-makers even top them if we look at "the big picture" with public education. Teachers are at the bottom, and students do not even appear on the chart! What if we changed our thinking and flipped the pyramid over, putting students at the top of the chart and teachers right beneath them? How would that change who drives instruction and how instructional decisions are made?

As I told my staff on the very first day I met with them, I would be right there beside them if we did what was right for the children. I have always believed children should be the foremost reason behind every decision made. Their intellectual, social, and emotional well-being must be what drives our desire as teachers and caretakers to do more and do better each and every day. As principal of my first school, I lived by this mantra in my daily practice and communicated it through my words and my actions. When I was appointed to open a new entrepreneurial school eight years later, this mantra became a part of our mission statement, and we were able to form our learning organization with the students at the top of our organizational chart. Here are some of the lessons I learned along the way:

Dream BIG

While creating a business plan for my entrepreneurial school, I envisioned a place where dreams were made and dreams came true, a place where students came first and every decision made was based on the best interests of the students. I decided my first theme would be "Building Dreams."

- **When creating a vision for your school, picture the students at the top of the organizational chart.** What would that look like? The students would be at the center of everything you do and every decision you make, and every decision you make would be based on the improvement of teaching and learning. Students are our customers! Teachers and staff members would form the next level on the chart, as they are our internal customers. You must take care of them as well because the well-being and morale of your staff directly affects the well-being and success of your students. Next come families and community members, whom you must also provide quality customer service. As you can predict, the local school board and state and federal departments of education would be at the bottom. Your school's board of directors, or leadership team, would make decisions on behalf of the students and other internal and external customers. Not your typical educational system organizational chart, is it?

- **The quality of the work we give students is directly related to the quality of the work students give us in return.** This idea of "working on the work and not on the student" is based on late author and thought leader Dr. Phillip Schlechty's "Working on the Work" (WOW) framework for creating quality work for students. This is not another program that comes with books and workbooks; it is a way of thinking about the work we give students and a framework for designing that work. Dr. Schlechty created the "Ten Critical Qualities of Student Work" to engage students in learning. These are: organization of knowledge, content and substance, product focus, clear and compelling standards, protection from adverse consequences for initial failures, affirmation of performance, affiliation, novelty and variety, choice, and authenticity. Dr. Schlechty looked at students as customers of knowledge work, teachers as leaders and designers of quality knowledge work, and principals as "leaders of leaders." He was also the first to differentiate the levels of student engagement found in classrooms. You can learn more about Dr. Schlechty's work at www.schlechtycenter.org.

I was proud to be selected as one of forty principals across the state of Florida to work alongside Dr. Schlechty and the talented members of his organization, the Schlechty Center, as a trainer for WOW through the Florida District School Superintendent's Leadership Academy. Through meetings positioned in the five regions of the state, we helped facilitate Dr. Schlechty's Working on the Work framework to principals and district leaders in all sixty-seven counties, and they in turn brought the word back to their colleagues in their school districts. From there, many individual school districts requested the training locally. Somewhere during this process, I had a lightbulb moment that made me realize this was how I could make a difference in my school and with my teachers and students. One of the other forty principals selected happened to be principal of my high school feeder-pattern, or "Innovation Zone," as we called it. This led our group of schools to groundbreaking achievements and created a "Pre-K through Twelfth Grade Community of Learners."

- **At the end of each day, each child experiences success and values doing something he or she has never done.** This core concept is at the heart of the Working on the Work (WOW) framework, which holds that all children can learn more than they already are learning and meet with success. I extended this belief to include teachers and staff members as well, so everyone within the organization would end each day with having gained knowledge in some area and feeling successful. Providing a WOW experience for everyone involved became a daily goal for me as I began to craft my vision into reality. Even to the extent that when opening our new school, we wrote this concept into our mission statement and called our school the "WOW School of the Century." Tom Peters, business guru and author of *The Pursuit of WOW*, defines the WOW experience as "stepping out and standing out from the growing crowd of look-alikes." That is exactly what we wanted to achieve.

High Expectations for ALL Students

In order for each student to achieve his or her greatest potential, you must create a culture of high expectations for all students. Students should be given equal opportunity and not be subject to discrimination on the basis of age, color, disability, gender identity, gender expression, genetic information, marital status, national origin, race, religion, sex, or sexual orientation.

- **Create lofty goals for all students and watch them rise to your level of expectation.** Every child has strengths and talents that make them unique and worthy of enriched learning opportunities and praise. Not every child will arrive at the same answer at the same time or in the same way, so you should allow each child the time and attention they need to be successful. Defining what a quality product looks like and using a rubric that outlines the necessary standards to reach a high level of excellence constitute effective visual self-checks for students to use throughout the creative-learning process. Conferencing with individual students and giving them feedback along the way also makes them feel important and worthy of your suggestions and praise.

- **Teach students to BELIEVE in themselves, and let them know you believe in them.** Creating a "can-do" attitude as a school-wide culture is critical to overall school success. This should include a risk-free learning environment where students can make mistakes and continue to improve their work until they find answers or produce a quality product. You should also allow students the opportunity to make choices about their work—their topic, their method, or their work product—so that it is meaningful and sustaining. Keep students actively engaged in their work by challenging them to further exploration and making sure the work they do is interesting and authentic to them, not to you. Authentic student engagement pushes children to persist with their work until they reach a product with which they are satisfied and they (and you) consider "quality." These are a part of Dr. Schlechty's Ten Critical Qualities of Student Work and the Working on the Work (WOW) framework as stated in a previous section.

- **Teach teachers and staff to believe in themselves, and let them know you believe in them.** To reiterate because it is so important, the well-being and morale of the teachers and staff is directly related to the well-being and morale of the students. One of my area superintendents used to tell our group of principals, "If you don't feed the teachers, they'll eat the children!" This applies both literally and figuratively. As a principal, you do not control the salaries of the teachers and staff, as that happens through collective bargaining groups. So how do you reward them if you cannot give them a raise? Yes. Food is one way to do it, and you can pay for it through your parent-teacher association, local business-partner donations, or grants that allow food as a line item. Using the high school culinary programs in your community gives some of your former students a chance to come back and shine for former teachers by making a special breakfast or lunch in return for funding their programs. Another reward can be professional development of the teachers' choice, which takes place during the regular school/workday and not at night or on weekends. Treating teachers and staff members like other professions that build learning into their workday goes a long way to increase both professionalism and morale. Having lunch with colleagues off campus is the icing on the cake, as opposed to the usual thirty-minute lunch period that includes dropping off and picking up your class, a bathroom break, and choking down your food while at school.

A Safe and Happy Environment

Every parent's wish for their child is for them to be safe and happy at school, both physically and emotionally. As an elementary school principal, it was my goal to provide a safe, happy environment for everyone who crossed our threshold. Teachers and staff members also need an environment where they feel safe and are happy to come to work. Parents and community members should feel a welcoming environment as soon as they enter the front doors. These are some of the ideas and practices I put into place based on my learning:

- **Safety is the number-one priority!** Walt Disney's four keys to customer service are safety, courtesy, efficiency, and show. Safety must always be the priority in every decision and never sacrificed for another key. When surveying parents as to their priorities for their school, I found the number-one priority was always safety. The principal and other available adults should be out of the office and visible during arrival and dismissal times and throughout the school day. Informal classroom visits, going out of one's way to check on a child, or spending time talking to students in the cafeteria during lunchtime were just a few of the ways I enjoyed modeling a safe and happy environment as my priority.
- **A "tone of decency"** is the Coalition of Essential Schools' "Eighth Common Principle" and should be non-negotiable. Dr. Ted Sizer founded the Coalition of Essential Schools Organization after publishing his book, *Horace's Compromise*, in 1984. This school-reform initiative is based on "Ten Common Principles" to live by, of which "Tone of Decency" is number eight. This principle stressed the importance of respect, fairness, generosity,

tolerance, and trust for everyone and served to set the tone for the school and school community. Signs posted throughout the halls and in high-traffic areas of the school served as a reminder to students and adults alike. (See www.essentialschools.org)

- **A bully-free zone in classrooms and common-areas of the school** was one of the first initiatives to come through our Shared Decision-Making team as a school-wide discipline and motivation plan. It addressed how teachers, administrators, and families would work together on student-discipline issues. In the year 2000, after I was named National Distinguished Principal from our eight years of work at my first school, I was honored to meet Peter Yarrow in Washington, D.C. He was rolling out a new program for schools called Operation Respect, which featured Peter, Paul, and Mary's recording of a song called, "Don't Laugh at Me." I was in my second month of opening a new school with a population of students on the autism spectrum, so this program spoke to my heart. Fortunately, it spoke to the heart of my entire staff as well, and we immediately began to implement the program school-wide. One of everyone's favorite lessons was where the teacher holds a paper heart in his/her hand and crinkles the heart into a tight little ball while talking about how the negative things we say and do to each other hurt our hearts. When the heart unfolds, the damage is illustrated by all the cracks and wrinkles we see, and more that we do not see. Over the years, I was also able to share and recommend this outstanding program to other schools, bring Peter Yarrow to my district, and collaborate with a neighboring school system to offer his program's professional development to teachers and guidance counselors across both districts. (See www.operationrespect.org)

- **"A home away from home"** was an important concept in creating a school environment that was comfortable and caring to students, to teachers and staff, and to parents and families. Everyone wanted a place where they felt valued and cared about as they learned, taught, and advocated for the best school setting for the children. The key was providing a caring staff with whom students felt comfortable and safe in talking about their concerns. Again, it was essential that I modeled this in everything I said and did for students, staff, parents, and community members. That "Disney customer service" feeling needed to be evident as soon as anyone walked through the doors and into our front office. Treating everyone as an important guest also helped break down barriers and alleviate the uneasiness in those coming into our school for the first time. Through school climate surveys, I found that parents felt less anxious if they knew their children were happy and safe at school.

- **Matching students with teachers based on their teaching and learning styles** was another concept we explored and implemented through our shared decision-making process. It started with a group of teachers who wanted to attend a local workshop focused on Dr. Marie Carbo's National Reading Styles Institute and her strategies for helping struggling readers achieve greater learning gains. Dr. Carbo's experience included her role as a classroom teacher, a special-education teacher, and a leading quality researcher who focused on struggling readers' needs and strengths. Our entire staff learned much about the students and themselves, including how *not* to match a group of hyperactive students with a hyperactive teacher for an entire year! Thank goodness for our risk-free environment. Learning styles included visual, auditory, and kinesthetic strategies that helped personalize instruction based on students' individual strengths and preferences. Individualized learning for students is a challenge for teachers; however, teaching an entire classroom of students as the only method is less effective than small-group and one-to-one instruction. Remember the saying: "Every student can learn, just not on the same day in the same way."

- **Provide options and choices for parents**, such as multiage classrooms and/or teachers who "loop" with their students to the next grade level so there is instructional continuity for two years. Jim Grant's "Staff Development for Educators" (SDE) became another "hot topic" both teachers and parents wanted to learn more about. His "Childhood Is a Journey Not a Race" concept highlights the developmental stages of learning and the appropriate tasks for children at each age and each stage. It also places value on the importance of allowing each child time to grow and develop at their own rate through exploration, trial and error, and play. In multiage groupings, younger children can experience a higher level of cognitive and social skills with older groups of children, while the older groups can practice confidence and leadership skills as they assist and mentor their younger classmates. A sense of community develops as the children in this learning environment learn to respect each other as individuals and care for each other in this family of learners. Decreased discipline issues, increased attendance rates, and an overall increase in motivation for learning are also benefits of these groupings.

- **Create "schools within a school"** (often called houses), where teacher teams are grouped vertically from K–5, and students stay together within their vertical house to give them greater personalization in large schools. Teacher collaboration in planning instruction can be valuable in really getting to know a small group of students and their families throughout their elementary-school years. These vertical teacher teams plan together and allow students from different grade levels to work together on student teams, creating innovative projects based on their interests and choices. The teachers also come to know each student intellectually, socially, and emotionally over the years, so they become like a cohesive, caring family. Parents love the continuity of this configuration because they get to know a specific group of teachers, their expectations for the students, and their policies regarding things such as homework and volunteering.

- **Scheduling is a strategy to utilize time, space, people, resources, and technology** during the school day to maximize individual instruction and student success. Robert Canady's "Parallel Block Scheduling Model" is one way to reduce class size for teachers and students so that students needing more individualized or small-group instruction get help, while larger, more diverse groups of students attend enrichment labs where they experience hands-on exploratory learning. Extending instructional time periods benefits students not only in core subjects like reading, writing, and mathematics but also in special subject areas such as art, music, physical education, science, and technology. Special-subject-area teachers often feel like their content is an afterthought, with only thirty minutes of instruction allotted to their class periods. Take away the time for the students to arrive at their classrooms and settle in and then to clean up and prepare to leave, and you are lucky to get twenty consecutive minutes of instruction! Let's think out of the box, and instead of schedule-driven schools, why not curriculum-driven schools? What if special-subject-area teachers saw the same groups of students for nine days in a row, for example? Just think of the projects students could create during that time. Also think of the connections students would make as they reinforced what they learned in their classrooms with what they did in their specials. Scheduling can be a powerful tool, but it requires additional innovative planning and commitment between all teachers and administrators. (See www.schoolschedulingassociates.com.)

Lifelong Learners

Lifelong learning is defined as voluntary formal and informal learning opportunities throughout people's lives that foster continuous improvement in knowledge and skills, both personally and professionally. The key idea here is creating student learners who love to learn and who voluntarily make continued self-improvement throughout their lives.

- **Instill the love of learning in all students, teachers, staff, parents, and members of the school community outside of the school staff and parents.** Make connections for students between subject areas so what they are learning makes sense. If teachers plan together across curriculum-content areas, units of instruction can be created to reinforce the same concepts and skills in reading and social studies or in science and mathematics, for example. In a self-contained classroom, one teacher teaches all the content areas and can tie their instruction together, but through collaborative planning, all teachers can expand their personal ideas and build units of instruction using many minds. If there are additional teachers of the arts or sciences, their inclusion in planning can multiply the impact of students making those connections.

Allow students the opportunity to ask questions and then explore learning on their own, or with teams, to find answers. Students are motivated to research information using technology because everything is so accessible and immediate. Adding the opportunity to work with their peers allows them to share their findings and increase their knowledge and expand their viewpoints. This is an example of the design quality affiliation.

Make connections for students between what they are learning and the real world. Invite a parent or community professional to come and speak about or demonstrate an area of expertise that connects with what the students are learning in class. Arrange distance learning or Skype to broaden those connections across the country or the world. The possibilities are endless!

Expose students to a variety of ways of learning so they can choose one that is interesting, exciting, and satisfying to them. The design qualities of choice and novelty and variety come into play here. Allow students choices in the subject area, the product, or the method of presenting their work. Use these strategies at all levels, and apply the same process to teachers and staff as learners, as well as parents and the community as learners. Design staff-development activities to mirror student activities using the design qualities of affiliation, novelty and variety, and choice. Hold parent nights in several content areas and include their children so they can learn how to learn together. Use the same design qualities of affiliation, novelty and variety, and choice so that students become the experts for their families and so everyone learns.

Active engagement at all levels of your organization will create a culture of love of learning, and above all, make learning fun!

- **Declare your school a learning organization,** and then set the standard or rubric by which you will assess your progress and hold yourself accountable. I used Dr. Phillip Schlechty's Images of School as my rubric as I created my vision of what my school as a learning organization would look like. One of the most common school images the public thinks of is the Factory Model. In this model, the student is "the product" of the assembly line of school K–12. The teacher is a skilled worker who "works on the student," and the principal is the shop foreman who oversees the workers and their products. The parent is the product supplier. The profile of the classroom is passive, as the students are expected to sit and absorb information until they understand, but not necessarily remember long-term. Testing, remediation, and more testing is the core business model used to report results. One of my favorite illustrations of this model is the famous "Lucy and the Chocolate Factory" episode of the *I Love Lucy* show. Lucy and Ethel get caught up in trying to wrap all the chocolates exactly alike, and then the foreman turns up the speed of the conveyor belt, as well as the pressure. Lucy wants to do a good job but cannot keep up, so the chocolates (or students) fall through the cracks.

  Another model of school the public is familiar with is the Hospital Model. Here the student is the patient, and the teacher is clinician, diagnostician, performer, and presenter. The teachers job is to "fix" the patient. The principal is the chief of staff, the parent is the questionable ally, and diagnosis, prescription, and treatment are the core business model. The classroom profile is well managed as the students analyze, apply, and follow their prescription so they can be "released," or graduate.

  The image of school as a Learning Organization Model is much different and one that supports the culture of lifelong learning. The student is a knowledge worker and volunteer for that work. The teacher is a leader and designer of quality work and a guide for instruction. The principal is the leader of leaders. The parents are members of the school community and partners in the educational process. The classroom profile is highly engaged, and the students' levels of learning include creating, evaluating, analyzing, applying, understanding, and remembering. The core business of the Learning Organization Model is designing engaging, intellectually demanding work for students and leading them to success in that work.

- **Dr. Phillip Schlechty's Working on the Work (WOW) framework** in action created a lifelong learning focus in my schools. How did I present the framework to my staff to encourage interest and discussion? By explaining that this framework was not another program to adopt and learn but a way of thinking about how students learn, and by sharing the Ten Design Qualities teachers can use to adapt the content mandated by the state when designing quality work for their students. And by asking, "What causes students to be engaged with the work they do?" and "Does this relate to students at the primary and secondary levels?" and "How does this apply to students with special needs and/or disabilities?"

It was always important to me to ask for volunteer teachers who would like more information and who were willing to try out the concepts without fear of repercussion or retaliation, and then provide continuous follow-up with those volunteers, discussing results, both positive and negative. When the teachers were ready to present what they'd learned to both small and large groups of peers and invite others into their classrooms to see their work in action, I gave them the time and opportunity to do so. This was the action plan upon which they came to a consensus as teachers:

> ★ **To design, create, and invent high-quality, intellectually demanding work for ALL students.** This meant teachers agreed to use Schlechty's design qualities as a framework for designing knowledge work that would engage all students to persist with their work until it was a quality product.

- **To facilitate the access of knowledge through a variety of sources.** Instead of lecturing and feeding students the information, teachers would act as facilitators and help students access the desired knowledge through the use of technology and experts, in addition to traditional books and print materials.
- **To change the delivery of information to include technology.** Teachers would learn to use computers, smartboards, distance learning, and all the technology available to them in their delivery of information to their students.
- **To coach, encourage, assist, and advise their students.** Again, the teacher's role would change to one of coach, assistant, adviser, and facilitator to students and their learning.

One of my kindergarten teachers explained the process as the role of the teacher was no longer to be the sage on the stage but the guide on the side.

Relationships

As you may have noticed by now, the end of each of my chapters has a pattern of the importance of relationships because I feel so strongly about developing connections between people. The Working on the Work (WOW) framework defines the rules, roles, and relationships of people and what that should look like. Some examples are:

- **The Student–Teacher Relationship**
  Why is the teacher so tired at the end of the day and the students go skipping out the door? Is the teacher spending most of the day lecturing or imparting knowledge? The student should be doing the work, and the teacher should be designing the work and facilitating the learning process. Students should be the customer or "volunteer" for the work they are "encouraged" to do. Instead of "the sage on the stage," the teacher should be "the guide on the side." Ted Sizer and the Coalition of Essential Schools called this relationship "student as worker and teacher as coach."

- **The Student–Student Relationship**
  Students should be learning to work together cooperatively to solve problems. Cooperative learning is a learning process of its own that prepares students for the real world of work. Students should be actively engaged in their learning, both hands-on and "minds-on." The work should be genuine and authentic to the student's current world of interests and importance; it's so important that students persist and derive satisfaction from their work and their work product. Teachers facilitate this process by teaching their students cooperative learning and by allowing each student to play the role of leader, recorder, timekeeper, and presenter. Teachers also design the work tasks that cause the students to use critical and creative thinking as well as manipulate objects or information sources to create their work product. The authenticity of the work is derived through the use of the design qualities of affiliation, novelty and variety, and choice.

- **The Teacher–Parent Relationship**
  The parent is the child's first teacher, hence parents know their children best. Teachers should listen to the parent's knowledge of the child without judgment, noting the similarities and differences they see in the classroom. Teachers are professionals with training in both subject-area knowledge and knowledge of the developmental ages and stages of children. Parents should listen to the teacher's expectations of learning content and social/emotional behavior in the classroom. Respect from both sides is essential in this relationship, the parents from the home and the teacher from the school. Both the parent and teacher are there for the same reason—the best interest of the child.

  Getting the parent to come to the school has become increasingly difficult because of their fear of losing time on their job or because they're working multiple jobs because of societal demands. What I have found that works is creating incentives for parents to come to school to conference with their child's teachers. Students receiving a homework pass or a free ice cream from the cafeteria can be enough to motivate the parent to make their child happy. Holding conference times at alternative hours such as evenings or weekends can be arranged by trading extra hours with teachers on planning days. We found that one of the most successful practices was to hold a portfolio conference night and involve the students in sharing their work portfolios with their families.

- **The School–Parent Relationship**
Parents and guardians should play an active role in their child's education. They should be invited to take part in activities for learning and learn strategies to use at home with their children. Parents often feel uncomfortable in the school setting because of their own past experiences. It is important for the school to present a welcoming, customer-focused environment to break down any preconceived barriers. Schools should do everything possible to create a collaborative atmosphere, asking questions about the student and asking for suggestions from the parent, before saying what should be done and how. Again, parents should know that school staff are professionals and have experience with how students learn, so they also need to be open to suggestions from the teacher and staff.

> *"Relationships are all there is. Everything in the universe only exists because it is in relationship to everything else. Nothing exists in isolation. We have to stop pretending we are individuals that can go it alone."*
> —Margaret J. Wheatley

The Theme Queen: Using Metaphors for Educational Change

Change is a process, not an event; a journey, not a destination. In organizational-change management, change is defined as getting from point A to point B with a transition period in between. There are many business models of the change process, including top-down, bottom-up, and more collaborative models. Educational change often means educational reform. Michael Fullan, author and worldwide authority on educational reform, says, "There are seven core premises that underpin our use of change knowledge." They are:

1. a focus on motivation (moral purpose, capacity, resources, peer and leadership support, and identity),
2. capacity building, with a focus on results (the collective effectiveness of a group raising the bar and closing the gap of student results),
3. learning in context (on the job, in the classroom, modeling new practices and behaviors),
4. changing context (sharing outside the school and across schools),
5. a bias for reflective action (not only learning by doing but by thinking about what you are doing),
6. tri-level engagement (in the school and community, in the district and in the state), and
7. persistence and flexibility for staying the course (sustainable and cultivated over time).

The first premise of motivation is the catalyst for change and is supported by the other six premises which are all about motivation and engagement. (See www.michaelfullan.ca)

Each spring, to set the tone for the upcoming school year, I would begin working on a school-wide theme that would guide the direction for our work. For example, for my first full year as principal, we started with "Focus on the Stars," which was designed to build confidence and a feeling of importance and personal value in both staff and students. I personally glittered each staff member's name on a gold foil star for their "dressing room" (classroom), and my dynamic assistant principal and I wore tuxedos and valet parked everyone's cars when they arrived the first day. To welcome them back for our first full school year together, we sent invitations two weeks before they were scheduled to return, to "invite" them back for their first planning day. The invitations were in the form of a ticket for act I of our yearlong production. Our Parent-Teacher Association (PTA) prepared an amazing welcome-back breakfast, including a chocolate fountain, for all our "cast members," followed by a meeting in the media center to "set the stage" for the coming school year. The front office and support staff even sang our own rendition of "Everything's Coming Up Roses" to paint a picture of our vision for the future success we would achieve, and we presented everyone with a long-stemmed red rose.

Unfortunately, Hurricane Andrew hit Miami, forty-five miles to our south, the morning the teachers and staff were to return. Fortunately, our school system was only affected by wind, rain, and debris from trees, so the teachers and staff returned the following day. As you can imagine, everyone's mind was not on school but on those families not so far away who had suffered extreme loss of property and possessions and had to relocate and find food and shelter. We adjusted our agenda to include time for talking and planning relief efforts for those to our south, but for the most part, we accomplished our goals for the day. As they say in the business, "The show must go on!"

This first year together, we changed attitudes and behaviors, built relationships of trust, and created and implemented a school-wide motivation and discipline plan that provided more time for teachers to teach and students to learn.

School-Wide Motivational Themes and the Process of Change

Each consecutive year, our themes became more related to where we were in the change process as a learning organization. Here are a few examples from the other years at my first school:

- **"Charting Our Course"** was our second school-wide theme using the metaphor of compasses in navigating the dark waters of change and setting a course for the development of our strategic plan. That year, each teacher and staff member received a passport with their welcome-aboard invitation. An archway of balloons covered the "gangway to the bridge," and cups of juice with little umbrellas were presented to each person as they came aboard anticipating a year of smooth sailing. The office and support staff sang a rendition of "On the Good Ship Lollipop," and the boatswain's whistle called for all aboard! My presentation was adapted from my Disney Institute training, which began with a picture of a five-pointed star labeled PARADIGM, PURPOSE, PEOPLE, PROCESS, and PLACE to represent the five aspects of CHANGE. For the first point, we reviewed the concept of PARADIGM shifts, or the way we view the world, something we'd learned through our shared decision-making activities the prior year. The second point noted there should be a PURPOSE for change, and a focus, not just change for the sake of changing. The third point showed that change involves PEOPLE, using individual talents and styles as well as teamwork involving interaction and conversation between those people. Point number four explained that change is a PROCESS; it takes time, knowledge, and patience, and it does not happen overnight. People must listen to each other and work together for change to be successful. Finally, the fifth point, the PLACE for change, is our environment—our physical environment, which creates excitement and motivation for learning, and our feeling environment or climate, which is our home away from home, a safe place, where everyone can take risks without fear of failure.

Whenever we embark on a journey of change, it is important to remember three steps: "Honor the past," "Challenge the present," and "Look toward the future." "Honor the past" means to respect the history, values, and traditions that are important to the organization. For change to take place, the past does not need to be thrown away and forgotten; in fact, the opposite is true. We must hold in high esteem the principles that are treasured and timeless. "Challenge the present" means to seize the day, or carpe diem! There is no time like the present to challenge yourself and others to be lifelong learners using your creativity, your imagination, and every possible teaching moment that presents itself. Finally, "Look toward the future" means defining your vision, mission, and goals to include everyone in your learning organization regardless of color, creed, special needs, race, religious beliefs, or sexual orientation. ALL CHILDREN CAN LEARN, no matter size or age, and that means all adults can learn too!

This theme set the tone for us to write our first mandated school-improvement plan, collectively embrace the process of change, and allow innovation and creativity to take place within our newly formed "culture of caring and support." Our first multiage classes became a reality, and everyone received professional development in identifying learning styles for our students. The number of student referrals and behavior incidents decreased drastically!

- **"Blazing New Trails,"** year three, found us hooking up our wagons on dusty, western trails and becoming "Paradigm Pioneers." Joel Barker, futurist and author of *The Business of Paradigms*, says, "The paradigm shift is the key ingredient in understanding change." A "paradigm shift" means fundamentally altering the way things are done. In his video of the same name, Barker says, "The future does not belong just to the people who create a paradigm shift. It belongs to pioneers—the people who are willing to accept high risk and open a new trail to the future. They put the new paradigm into practice." He uses the pioneers of the American West as an example of blazing new trails, mapping them, and making them safe for travel. He also warns of the dangers of "Settler Mentality" or accepting the status quo. According to Barker, paradigm pioneers possess these characteristics:

1. Intuition. The ability to make good decisions with incomplete information.
2. Courage. The willingness to move forward in the face of great risk.
3. A commitment of time. An investment for the long-term—no quick fixes!

And, yes, I am sure you've guessed by now that our "Blazing New Trails" theme included scrolls summoning teachers and staff "Wanted—Dead or Alive" at the OK Corral. Reward? Chow and WOW! Our song? Yep! "Back in the Saddle Again." Our setting? A Conestoga wagon borrowed from a local catering company, bales of hay, and a line-dance break to "Achy Breaky Heart." Wow! The celebration? A list of accomplishments, or trails already blazed. The call to action? To be Paradigm Pioneers, trust our intuitive judgments, have the courage to take a risk, and commit to the long-term for providing ALL students with a total quality environment of continuous improvement. Oh, and last but not least—HAVE FUN!

Dr. Phillip Schlechty's version of the pioneer story adds several other levels of adventurers: the trailblazers, who are willing to take great risks to move the work forward; the pioneers, who follow the trailblazers with increasing confidence and trust; the settlers, who wait for the pioneers to say "It's safe out here"; the stay-at-homes, who sit in their rocking chairs on the front porch and wait for the change to go away; and the saboteurs, who try to disrupt the change.

At the end of our third year, our "trailblazers" formed our first vertical team and provided parents with a choice of our "school within a school" concept, while our pioneers followed along with their new learning and innovation in their classrooms. We still had some convincing to do with our "stay-at-homes," and we had not yet identified any saboteurs. Our teachers administered a learning-styles inventory to every student and began to personalize instruction for each student.

- **"Winning with Teamwork"** was our school-wide theme for year four. We drafted our student players and teacher coaches to training camp, adjusted our strategic game plan to include the new Florida Sunshine State Standards, and coached each other to create winning teams and students! Don Shula and Ken Blanchard's new book, *Everyone's a Coach,* served as the motivating force for a simple acronym (COACH) used to push effective leaders to greatness:

    C   Conviction-driven: never compromise your beliefs
    O   Overlearning: team practice until perfect
    A   Audible-ready: know when to change your game plan
    C   Consistency: respond predictably to performance
    H   Honesty-based: high integrity, straightforward, "walk your talk"

The Coalition of Essential Schools' principles of "teacher as coach" and "student as worker (player)" served to reinforce our message of rules, roles, and relationships. Parents and community members became our "raving fans" as defined in another book by Ken Blanchard, which defined one of our major goals of revolutionary customer service! "Take Me Out to the Ball Game" was our opening song, and living in South Florida, we coordinated a school family night where we were recognized at a Miami Marlins baseball game and even managed to have a student assembly featuring players from the Miami Dolphins!

By the end of year four, we had solidified successful teaching teams who'd designed quality work for their students. We unpacked the Florida Sunshine State Standards as a staff so everyone would know the expectations for students at every grade level and how they progressed from kindergarten through the fifth grade. Students became more accountable for their work, teachers facilitated and coached, and our families and community were pleased with the customer service they received.

- In year five, **"Engaging the Next Generation,"** we boarded the *Starship Excellence* and traveled at warp speed into the new state phenomenon of giving schools letter grades to hold us accountable. This would be the first year the Florida Comprehensive Assessment Test (FCAT) would be field tested. Fasten your seat belts! Our invitation was a RED ALERT for all Starfleet officers to report to the bridge for the maiden voyage of the USS *Excellence* and to prepare to be beamed into the twenty-first century. Our mission:

> To explore strange new worlds.
> To seek out civilizations.
> To boldly go where no one has gone before.
> Our flight plan: the Q (quality) continuum
> COMMUNICATE! ENGAGE! and MAKE IT SO!

Dr. Meg Wheatley's *Leadership and the New Science* book and video set the tone for how we were feeling about the chaos we were expecting to experience with our new state law on grading schools. Through discoveries in quantum physics, biology, and chaos theory, Dr. Wheatley showed us how to deal successfully with change and uncertainty in our organizations and lives. Some powerful reflections included:

> ORDER can emerge out of chaos.
> INFORMATION informs us and forms us.
> RELATIONSHIPS are all there is.
> VISION is an invisible force field.

On a lighter note, our opening song was our rendition of "In the Year 2525," projecting our vision of school to the future, followed by "Rocket Plan" ("Rocket Man"), "Blue Moon," and "Here Comes the Sun" throughout the school year. Also in 1996, over $2 billion in federal grants became available in the Technology Literacy Challenge Fund, a program that challenged public schools to make computers available to every student. The world was changing.

Computer technology and the internet became an increased motivation for learning for students, teachers, and staff members. Our innovation zone, or feeder pattern of schools, created a technology team K–12. Star Trek taught us life lessons about celebrating diversity as our "neighborhood" began to change demographically. Our students took the field test for the Florida Comprehensive Assessment Test (FCAT), and we now knew what to expect and how to hone our test preparation for our students.

- **"Engineering Change": 21st Century Express:** In our sixth year, we boarded an Amtrak train in the morning and traveled one and a half hours north to Okeechobee, Florida, for lunch at a quaint country restaurant, returning by bus later that afternoon. "Why?" you ask. A captive audience, a change of scenery, a celebration of our work well done? Well, all of the above and, of course, if you are going to run your own 21st Century Express train all year, you'd better have experienced the adventure with all your senses! Many staff members had never experienced a train ride—grassy fields passing quickly by the windows, the click-clack sound of the tracks, the whistle calling all aboard, the smell of coffee and pastries from the snack car. We asked tough questions on that day, such as "Where are you on the change train?" and "Are you the engine with a clear vision and direction, ready to speed ahead, or are you the saboteur lying down on the tracks attempting to stop the train so that everyone will get off and the change process will crash and burn?" This metaphor created a sense of urgency and an expectation for everyone to come aboard the "change train" and buy in to the Working on the Work (WOW) framework. Research says it takes five to seven years for organizational change to take place. After five years, we had made significant progress on our action plan, and were "on track" with student achievement as well as transforming the climate and culture of our school into one of a learning organization. It was time for the remaining settlers and stay-at-homes to make a commitment for the common good. This would be the first year that all students in grades four, five, eight, and ten would take the state FCAT, although this year would be considered the baseline data by which we would be measured in the future. "WE KNOW WE CAN" was our mantra! The song "I've Been Working on the Railroad" became "I've Been Working on the Work," and "The Locomotion," "Five Hundred Miles," and "There's a Light at the End of the Tunnel" from *Starlight Express* gave us the fuel we needed to meet the state mandates for testing.

All aboard the 21st Century Express! Year six gave us our baseline data for FCAT and a commitment from our entire staff to become "pioneers" for change.

- **"Safari to Success":** Year seven was "a quality expedition" of discovering what quality teaching and learning looks like. Our staff field trip took us to Lion Country Safari, where our office and support staff dressed as lions and zebras and elephants (Oh, my!) and sang "Circle of Life" from the *Lion King*. Our toolkits included binoculars to help us focus on our goals, cameras to take snapshots of learning to assess our students, and safari hats to shade us from the harsh public sunshine that would publish our test results for all the world to see! Our teacher learning communities would be in full swing for the year, and our technology plan would help us collect the data we needed to guide our students to success. Teachers were comfortable visiting each other's classrooms, the classrooms of other teachers in our Innovation Zone K–12, and even classrooms across our school district. We would take this year to stop and reflect on all our accomplishments, sharpen the art and craft of our teaching, and refine our preparation for FCAT based on our previous year's baseline data.

- **"Motoring Minds into the Millennium":** Year eight began with our first real FCAT results. In reading, 73 percent of our students met the minimum criteria; in math, 81 percent met the minimum criteria; and in writing, 56 percent met the minimum criteria, which was a higher standard. The minimum criteria (school grades C, D, and F) was 60 percent achieving a level 2 or above in reading and math, and 50 percent receiving a level 3 in writing. The criteria for a school grade of A or B was 50 percent of students scoring a level 3 or above in reading and math, and 67 percent scoring a level 3 or above in writing. Our school grade was a C. We knew we had work to do, and we had a plan for effective instructional alignment, effective use of instructional time, and data analysis and data-based decision-making to get us to "the checkered flag" at the finish line. So we put our pedals to the medal, fired all cylinders, created a sense of urgency, and headed for the A+ victory lane!

  This was also the year I accepted two awards on behalf of my awesome, hardworking, and very caring staff: the Florida Commissioner's Award for Outstanding Leadership, and the U.S. Department of Education's National Distinguished Principal from Florida. Yes! I was going to Disney World and to the Department of State in Washington, D.C. I was so proud of my school's teachers, staff, parents, and community and what they had accomplished over the past seven years, I could burst! I was also appointed principal of a brand-new school being built in my city and would move on as a planning principal for the new school in March. Even as I moved on, I was confident we had built the capacity to achieve an A grade at the end of the year, and we did!

Positive School Climate and Culture

I attributed my school's success to the creation of a positive school climate and culture as the foundation upon which everything else was built. Let's review what a positive school climate and culture looks like:

- **A positive school climate** embodies the qualities and atmosphere that affect the attitudes and behavior of all shareholders. School should be a welcoming place where entering the front office you receive a warm greeting from the staff and feel like you are the most important person in the room. The first impression is the only impression. It should reflect the high morale of the students, staff, parents, and community members. A tone of decency must be felt through respectful, nonjudgmental behaviors from everyone you meet. Communication is open and honest and ongoing between and among all parties involved. Students model positive behavior resulting from the positive and motivational discipline plan that is in place. There should be sensitivity to diversity shown at all times.

- **A positive school culture** is a way of life based on what the school stands for—a vision that embodies the core values and purposes and that channels staff and students in the direction of successful teaching and learning. Collegiality and teamwork abound. A safe environment is in place that encourages experimentation, innovation, and risk-taking. There are high expectations for ALL students, staff, parents, and community members. An air of trust and confidence is evident in all interactions. Everyone is shown appreciation and recognized for their contributions to the school and learning organization. There is a continuity of caring and an atmosphere of daily celebration and humor. A positive school climate and culture is the most important foundation a school can have in being able to reach their highest potential for teaching and learning.

- **Quality customer service** must be modeled for both internal and external customers from the top down through interpersonal skills. Learn from the best! The Ritz Carlton's motto is "We are ladies and gentlemen serving ladies and gentlemen." Disney "creates magical moments for guests of all ages." Jet Blue's mission is "to inspire humanity both in the air and on the ground." Then there is "The Nordstrom Way of branding their customer service by empowering employees to use their best judgment." The ultimate goal of customer service is emotional engagement—causing others to want to be there, anticipating the next event or interaction with them, and feeling like you are a part of something bigger than yourself that makes a difference in the lives of others. You must consistently communicate "your school's way" to all stakeholders. This creates a "brand" for your school, your expectations, and the way you do business; for example, "The ABC School Way."

Creating Anticipation and Excitement through Out-of-the-Box Thinking

Remember at the beginning of this chapter when I defined the educational change process?

At the top of the list of the seven core premises was motivation. The other six premises support the first and are all about motivation and engagement. This was how I put these into practice:

- **Our school-wide themes** resulted in everyone looking forward to the coming school year. Parents were as excited as their students to discover the new theme, buy their T-shirts, and volunteer for events and in the classrooms, and the students loved having their parents taking part in their school experience. Teachers were excited to decorate their classrooms and design their instruction to include connections to the new theme. Many met during the summer to plan, shop, and create their magical classroom learning environment to welcome their students back. The welcome-back celebration for the teachers and staff was based on sights, sounds, ideas, and experiences for the new theme and carried over to the students' welcome-back celebrations as well. We planned field trips, enrichment activities, and family nights to support the theme and focused learning for the year.

- **Engaging everyone in the experience** was critical, so everyone had a role and a purpose. For example, "Winning with Teamwork"

positioned students as players, teachers and staff as coaches, and parents and community as cheerleaders, boosters, and raving fans. Each year, the front office and support staff dressed in theme clothing and sang songs to welcome the staff back and set the tone for the year ahead. The teachers and staff looked forward the welcome-back invitations they received, which set expectations and gave them hints about their first day of focused learning. Parents and community partners gave a welcome-back breakfast and provided treats to kick off our school-wide celebration of success. We decorated the school office, main hallways, and cafeteria to motivate students and to reflect the theme for the year. The parent-teacher association provided T-shirts with our school logo and theme to sell to the school community as a fundraiser for the students.

- **Exhibitions of quality work affirmed the importance of our students' work to the community at large.** One of Schlechty's Working on the Work (WOW) design qualities is "Affirmation of Performance." Students naturally enjoy positive feedback on their work from their teachers, parents, and peers, but extending an invitation to business and community members to come to the school and classrooms in person takes that feedback to the next level. Student-led conferences were one of the opportunities where grade levels would invite families to take part in a nighttime classroom setting where each student would present their work portfolio to their family and explain what they had learned. This started at the first-grade level! School-wide exhibitions occurred twice a year and included performances in art, music, science, social studies, and movement, as well as quality student work products adorning every wall in every hallway throughout the school. Sometimes the students acted as docents in a famous museum and would explain the artwork or the unit of study they had just completed. These exhibitions were examples of performance-based, authentic assessments and deeper learning instead of only a state FCAT test that gave a snapshot of one day in the life of a child. One of the greatest compliments we repeatedly received was how our school reflected a student-centered environment for teaching and learning.

- **The Integration of Technology.** The 1990s was the decade additional computers were added to schools through federal and state grant monies. The internet also became available to the public, and schools became wired or "retrofitted" to receive signals from other computers around the world and share information on the World Wide Web. At our school, there were teachers who were excited about using computers for instruction in their classrooms, and then there were those who weren't so excited, so we created a technology plan that included a team of teachers we empowered to become technology trainers. We also integrated technology with our reading, writing, and math family nights for parents and students to learn together. Our tech-savvy assistant principal created our school website, which informed parents and the community about school programs and events and won the highest honor from our state public relations association.

The new school I opened in 2000 came with a school-wide, state-of-the-art technology system. This included computers in every classroom, a technology lab, distance-learning equipment, a sound system, and a TV studio where our students broadcasted a live news show into every classroom each morning to start the day! Every school should have the latest equipment to enhance and support content and student learning.

Relationships

"The quality of your life is the quality of your relationships."
—Anthony Robbins

Building Positive Relationships in Diverse Communities

In the year 2000, I had the unique opportunity to apply for a brand-new school currently under construction in my same city. The school would join parts of three school communities that were critically overcrowded, one being an exceptionally wealthy school community, the other two more diverse. The parents of those children being displaced and reassigned to the new school felt a lot of anxiety. The school ethnicity would be approximately one-third white, one-third black, and one-third Hispanic, with about 3 percent Asian and 3 percent multiracial. Fifteen percent of the school population was denoted as "English speakers of other languages" (ESOL) who combined spoke a total of fourteen different languages. Students with the designation "exceptional student education" (or students with special needs) made up 20 percent of the total students, including a new program for students with autism. More than 30 percent of the students would be below the poverty level, receiving free or reduced lunch.

I was officially named principal in March 2000 and left my first school to become a "planning principal" in a district office located in a nearby city. I could take my extremely qualified confidential secretary/office manager as my partner to help me achieve the daunting tasks coming our way. We visited the dusty construction site, donned our hard hats, and selected colors for our paint and tile. I was also granted an opportunity to submit a business plan so we could become a designated "entrepreneurial" school that was a state model for "innovation and school choice" and would give my school leadership team more autonomy in our decision-making processes and in hiring teachers and staff. My first hire was the best head facilities serviceperson in the business. The two of us worked with the construction crew to make sure nothing we needed as a facility fell through the cracks. My second hire was my assistant principal, who was an expert in curriculum and stayed at her current school until June but assisted me in personnel selection and curriculum decisions until then.

Through the District Personnel Department and teachers' union, we negotiated a memorandum of understanding that allowed teachers from all three school communities to *apply* for positions at the new school, without guarantee of a position because of seniority. For the balance of teachers and staff, I could recruit and hire from an application process throughout the district and beyond. During the interview process, I set the expectations for the teachers and staff based on the school's potential entrepreneurial status. I also was able to select my first leadership team of teacher-leaders for each grade level and content area and appoint them to their leadership roles. They also stayed at their current schools until the end of the school year but were excited and willing to participate in curriculum decisions and make choices on our instructional materials. My confidential secretary and I met with and interviewed the teachers at locations convenient to them after school. You could find us in the lobby of the local medical center and even in the mayor's conference room at city hall. We formed partnerships, built relationships, and utilized every opportunity to involve the community in every way possible. I was convinced that I had hired the "best of the best" teachers for every subject area, teacher assistants for designated classrooms, and non-instructional personnel to support everyone else. The most exciting part of the process was that they all *wanted* to be there!

I attended all three of the existing schools' meetings with parents and community members to welcome them to their new school, answer any questions they had, and communicate future meeting dates. We held these meetings at the city performing arts center's community room, which was directly across the street from the school. As teachers and staff came on board, they joined the community meetings and became a part of the total decision-making process. I was the facilitator of our tasks, which included voting on a school name, a mascot, and colors, which all had to be approved by the school board before summer and finalized for our opening in August. The parent-teacher associations from the three schools had to meet, organize, and select officers for the new school based on the families who would be attending. Our board of directors, which included teachers, staff, and parent-leaders, met regularly to keep the lines of communication flowing.

It was during this organizational time I decided that the perfect theme for the first year at our new school was "Building Dreams." So, in keeping with my themes tradition, our front office and support staff wore plastic hard hats, neon-orange vests and tool belts, and sang our version of YMCA which was "W-O-W" for our 'WOW School of the Century" and our core business, Working on the Work. We had our dream school and hired our dream team, who all wanted to be there and had bought in to our entrepreneurial plan. We were ready to design and create quality work for students so we could get quality work from them in return. From that point on until I retired in 2013, our themes were all about continuing the dream.

Building Positive Relationships

Relationships have been a reoccurring theme throughout each chapter of this book. I have a passion for building positive relationships with all stakeholders in my school community, both internally and externally. This was extremely critical in bringing three diverse school communities together to form our new school community. This is how we began the process:

- **Defining roles** was an important piece that was carefully and strategically thought out in our planning process. The organizational chart for our business model defined the way we conducted our "core business." Students were at the top of the organizational chart!

The next tier was the board of directors, which consisted of teachers, staff, parents, and community leaders, along with myself as the school principal. Our school leadership team came next, followed by teachers and staff, parent groups, business and community partners, the school board, and finally, the Florida Department of Education. Wow, is that flipping the pyramid or what?

- **Parent and school partnerships** included a Parent-Teacher Association that would act as student advocates at the local, state, and national levels; organize family activities at school; and serve as our fundraising agent. The School Advisory Council was made up of a specific group of people mandated by the state but selected by the groups they served. An example of this was a representative of the teachers' union and a cross-section of teachers, staff, parents, and community members. Their role was to actively create and monitor a school improvement plan and approve a school budget. The School Advisory Forum was a district initiative that involved the parents and community at the school and district levels and dealt with issues such as safety, legislation, and facility needs at each of those levels. Volunteers were a very important part of the home–school connection and added extra sets of helping hands in the classrooms, cafeteria, at school events, and even at home, making phone calls or preparing materials for class projects. Everyone who volunteered at a school had to pass a rigorous district screening that included fingerprinting and a criminal background check. Remember, our number-one priority was always safety!

- **Local business and government support:** We established partnerships with local businesses that had a stake in our school families and community. Often it is tempting to only go for the big brands that have more money to offer. However, through the years we discovered the value of a family night at a family-owned pizza restaurant or ice cream parlor. Those times brought us more than money. We supported small businesses and families in our school community, contributed to and promoted our local economy, and ultimately scored priceless publicity for our school. We even developed a WOW directory of the parents and families of our students who were self-employed plumbers, mechanics, electricians, and air-conditioning specialists who could provide services to other families to build a true sense of community.

The fact that the school itself was built on land donated to the school board by the city opened many doors to engaging city officials in our important work. As I mentioned previously, we held teacher and staff interviews in conference rooms at city hall and at the city medical center, and we held organizational meetings in public meeting rooms at the city performing arts center. In addition, we conducted our off-site emergency-evacuation drills at the city park across the street; at public safety buildings, including the police and fire departments; and at the city gymnasium—all within walking distance. Our school was really the best kept neighborhood secret, which we decided not to keep secret from the world!

- **District and state support** is crucial to your success. It is the foundation that supports your quality public school. Knowing your school-board members and inviting them to your school for innovative student activities and community events is good visibility for everyone involved. Knowing your state legislators through written contact is a good first step, but inviting them to personally observe quality teaching and learning in your classrooms can result in their having firsthand experiences when voting on critical educational issues. One state representative came to our awards ceremony at the end of each year to recognize one fifth-grade student for their service to the community and to present that student with a citizenship award affixed with the state seal.

In our early years of operation, two of our fifth-grade classes presented a production of *American History and the Civil War*. It was the culmination of their unit of study and included costumes and props, both authentic and replicas, created and provided by the students' families. It was authentic engagement in learning at its best, followed by a feast of food representative of this historical era. During the performance, the classes displayed both a Confederate as well as an American flag. The overall message of the production was that we must never forget humanity's mistakes of the past, so we do not repeat them in the future. The next thing we knew, district and state officials were at our door because we had displayed a Confederate flag and it had offended someone, and this was in 2000–2001, not 2017, where we saw these things in the news every day! We were thankful to have built meaningful relationships at the district and state levels as those involved knew our work as a school and were able to help us through this uncomfortable but valuable learning experience.

Understanding Diverse Cultures

As I stated in the opening paragraph of this chapter, our school reflected a wide diversity of cultures. The ethnicity was approximately one-third white, one-third black, and one-third Hispanic, with fifteen percent of the school's population speaking a total of fourteen different languages. Twenty percent of the total were students with special needs and more than thirty percent of the students were below the poverty level. This presented challenges as we sought to understand the diverse cultures we served and to make every student and family feel welcome at our school.

- **Valuing diversity** meant identifying each student as unique, with individual characteristics, beliefs, and cultural backgrounds. Each student was different and had value in the multicultural society we lived in, as well as in the democratic process. Sometimes we know this on a philosophical level, but do we really dig deep for understanding? Multicultural education had been a part of school curricula for a decade, but we found ourselves celebrating "Black History Month," "Hispanic Heritage Month," and "Students with Disabilities Awareness Month," as if these differences only happened one month out of the school year!

This was a time and opportunity to take diversity to another level and put all our differences on the table. We offered diversity training for staff and parent groups to help everyone become familiar with cultural differences and to quell any sensitivities to behaviors that, without knowledge of a particular culture, might be uncomfortable or offensive. Language support for students and families whose first language was not English also helped break down any communication barriers lost in the translation process. Matching students with staff or older student "buddies" who spoke the same language helped relieve fear of being in an unfamiliar place. One of the challenges we continually faced was ensuring that our staff was a representation of the diverse culture of our students, families, and the community we served.

- **Being human** is one thing we all have in common. We thought, "Let's begin with our commonalities and then move to our differences." This began a series of "Courageous Conversations about Diversity and Race," with an esteemed colleague and skilled facilitator from outside our school asking tough questions and helping us dig deeper in understanding, respecting, and valuing each other as human beings. We felt it was important to initiate and model this process as adults, then pass it on to our students. In the new millennium after 9/11, there was much work to be done. One of our new, shared values became "There is only one race, and it is THE HUMAN RACE." One of the essential driving forces of discovery was the question "What does it mean to be human?" It was a beginning.

Relationships

"If civilization is to survive, we must cultivate the science of human relationships—the ability of all peoples, of all kinds, to live together, in the same world, in peace."
—Franklin D. Roosevelt

Who's Running the Schoolhouse?

Over the past twenty years, the focus of public education has changed dramatically. Instead of basing instructional decisions on the developmental needs of children and the quality training and development of teachers, the emphasis has shifted to the importance of creating high-stakes standardized tests and a national curriculum to teach to those tests, called the Common Core State Standards. Of course, competitive bids had to go out to companies who could develop those tests. This resulted in millions of dollars spent on lobbying by those same companies at both the state and federal government levels. Thus began the national corporate school-reform movement, which has made some corporations and entrepreneurs multi-billionaires while creating distrust in public schools and the people who have the experience and expertise to run them.

Decisions Are Not Made by Those with Experience and Expertise

- **Why aren't teachers and administrators in public schools making the decisions about how children should be learning?** Teachers must have at least a bachelor's degree in education, and many have their master's degrees and further specialization and have received certification by the states to teach their subject content areas. Teachers who teach preschool and kindergarten must have a separate certification in early childhood education. Teachers who teach special education students must have an added certification in the specific area of special needs they teach. All teachers and administrators must have mandated rigorous training components in strategies for English speakers of other languages (ESOL) students. Administrators must have at least a master's degree in school leadership or administration and a state and local certified program to advance from teacher-leader to assistant principal to principal. Both newly hired teachers and administrators have teams of highly experienced coaches and mentors who support them during their first year and longer. These certifications and programs signify the many years of study and practical, on-the-job experience these professionals have undertaken to hone their craft. Do you think they are qualified to make decisions about teaching and learning?

- **Legislators and politicians are currently making the decisions** on how and what students will learn and how they will be tested on their knowledge and abilities. Ask yourself these questions:

  ⋆ Are legislators' and politicians' decisions driven by outside interests that have corporate and political influence with their constituents?

  ⋆ What involvement do these outside interests have with the legislators and politicians in their elections and in their decision-making?

  ⋆ Could the legislators and politicians pass the tests currently mandated for teachers or even for students?

In 1998, when Jeb Bush ran for Florida governor, the focus of his campaign was the "Opportunity Scholarship Program." This voucher program allowed for state funds to pay tuition at church-run schools. In 2006, the state supreme court found this to be unconstitutional. That same year, the Florida Senate refused Bush's request to put a constitutional amendment on the ballot to appeal the provision of separation of church and state. When Jeb Bush became governor in 1999, he signed legislation that mandated the state FCAT test and tied those scores to grading schools on an A to F scale. After leaving the governorship in 2007, Bush formed the educational think-tank Foundation for Educational Excellence, based in Tallahassee, Florida, the state capital. In his short run for president in 2016, ex-governor Bush touted his achievements in transforming Florida schools, but he never used the term "public schools."

In regard to his "school choice" agenda, he said, "The United States has over 13,000 government-run monopolies run by unions" as his reference to public schools. This showed bias against public schools and a preference for shifting public school monies to private and parochial schools.

- **Testing and evaluation companies that currently write the tests for students** in the state of Florida and other states across the country are now multibillion-dollar businesses. Pearson Education is the richest of this handful of companies, and they are based in the United Kingdom. The money currently being spent on standardized testing was previously spent on innovative programs, "per pupil allocations" or dollars given for materials and supplies for students, and teacher salaries. Teacher salaries in my Florida district in 2007 were $38,500 for a beginning teacher; $45,770 for a teacher with fifteen years of experience; and $70,000 for teachers at the top of the pay scale with twenty-one-plus years. In 2017, teacher salaries in my Florida district were $40,724 for a beginning teacher and $46,164 for a teacher with fifteen years of experience. The pay scale currently stops at fifteen years because teachers are no longer paid for years of experience but are paid for "performance" instead. Teachers can currently make an extra $3,650 per year for a master's degree or up to $8,000 for a doctorate degree. However, "pay for performance" means the teacher's salary is determined by the test scores of their students and the rating their administrator gives them on the current evaluation instrument. Those ratings can be "highly effective," "effective," or "needs improvement." Teachers who taught students who were not tested on the content area of their teaching (like art, music, or physical education) would be paid based on the performance of the "school scores" and grade and not on the quality of lessons that integrated reading, writing, math, social studies, and science into their area of instructional expertise. Bottom line? Teachers received no bonuses, no raises, and no "highly effective" ratings on their evaluations regardless of my administrative evaluations of the quality of their work.

Teacher evaluations have always been a part of identifying quality teachers, and I believe they should continue to be a part of constructive feedback, support, and assistance for all teachers. It is not the evaluation process teachers object to, it is the state process and secret formulas used.

Teacher evaluations are now also written by companies who are for-profit based, and the state formulas for rating teachers (value-added model or VAM) are convoluted and make no sense regarding the actual teaching and learning that takes place in the classroom. One of these profitable companies is Dr. Robert Marzano's Learning Sciences International based out of West Palm Beach, Florida. In 2007, Dr. Robert Marzano published a book, *The Art and Science of Teaching: A Comprehensive Framework for Effective Instruction*, which presents a model for ensuring quality teaching that balances the necessity of research-based data with the equally vital need to understand the strengths and weaknesses of individual students. Along with *Classroom Instruction That Works* and *The Highly Engaged Classroom*, Marzano's books are used by schools across the country to illustrate the evolution of effective teaching practices over time. Five years later, these valuable resources morphed into the new Marzano's Standards-Driven Causal Evaluation for teachers, which required administrators to see evidence of sixty specific instructional elements in a thirty- to forty-minute period that would result in student achievement in a standards-based classroom. This played right into the hands of the standards-based FCAT test and the test-focused learning environment that had become the new normal in public schools. The Marzano Framework for Effective Instruction was never designed to be used as an evaluation tool; it was designed to be a developmental learning tool for teachers to improve effective teaching practices over time. As an evaluation instrument, it does not allow a principal to use other criteria to determine a highly effective rating. For example, if a teacher is a district trainer in their content area, works with other teachers at the district and state levels to coach or model best practices, or has achieved a Teacher of the Year ranking at the district or state levels, there is no place on the teacher evaluation instrument to give credit for those achievements. It is strictly confined to the thirty- to forty-minute classroom observations.

My question is "Who is benefiting from these companies and the tests and evaluations they are paid to create?" In 2013, I decided to retire a bit earlier than I originally planned because my answer to this question was not "students" or "teachers" or the "learning organization" I had dedicated my life's work to achieve as the standard of quality. I could no longer be expected to grade or *de*grade teachers whose innovative lessons authentically engaged students in learning by picking apart sixty elements I may not have observed or deemed appropriate for that lesson. I personally had highly effective teachers who were leaders of other teachers in and beyond the schoolhouse, but that did not count toward my thirty- to forty-minute observation. It also did not account for a teacher's "pay for performance" ranking from the state, which was determined by the school's student scores in tested grades only, whether the teacher taught those students or that grade or not. That went against the very fiber of my being and my convictions of what was developmentally right for children and morally right for adults.

- **Corporate charter schools have become a way to privatize education** and make huge profits on the backs of our students and families. Current legislation at both the state and federal government levels favors for-profit corporate charter schools using taxpayer monies allocated for public schools. The belief is that "the money should follow the child." For example, in 2017, the state of Florida's legislature passed Florida Law CS/HB 7069, which includes an appropriation of $413, 950,000 in recurring general revenue funds and $5 million in nonrecurring revenue funds originally allocated for public schools to be used to establish "Schools of Hope." Under the guise of "school choice" for parents, for-profit corporate charter schools are being recruited to further expand in Florida. Although charter schools are "free" for students, the money for their operation is drained from public-school dollars. Charter schools in Florida are unregulated and do not have the same accountability standards or transparency as public schools. Few charter schools provide the same services to special-education students as do public schools, and teachers do not have to be certified in the areas they teach. In addition, major funders of this corporate reform movement include the Bill and Melinda Gates Foundation, the Eli Broad Foundation, and the Walton Family Foundation, who all support and underwrite the expansion of charter schools; test-based evaluation of teachers; and pay for performance, or merit pay. The Gates Foundation collaborated with Pearson Education to develop online curriculum to teach the Common Core Standards. As New York University professor and former U.S. Assistant Secretary of Education Diane Ravitch points out, "None of the main recipients of foundation funding are models for American Education." In her book *Reign of Error*, Ravitch goes on to explain that "corporate reformers want education decisions in the hands of a powerful executive who is immune to public opinion. They like the idea of a governor who appoints a commission to override the decisions of local school boards that resist charter schools. At the school level, they want principals and administrators who can hire and fire at will, without due process." That about sums it up.

The state does not mandate that corporate charter schools meet the same standards as public schools, and they do not have to hire highly qualified, certified teachers. The National Center for Education Statistics reported that in Ohio in 2010, charter school teachers made 59 percent of what public school teachers made. U.S. public school teacher salaries and benefits represent 89 percent of instructional costs, or $287 billion a year. If all schools in Ohio were privatized and teachers were paid the charter-school rate, the corporations could make a difference of $118 billion in profit. The same report showed that in Michigan, charter schools cut instruction money by $1,140 per student, raised their administrative costs by $774 per student, and still came out ahead by $366 per student. Multiply that by the 55.4 million K–12 students, and privatization would yield a potential profit of $20 billion. Staggering figures, to say the least! A young teacher who joins a powerful charter-school network and rises on the fast-track career ladder can quickly be managing his or her own charter school or assume leadership roles in large urban districts or state departments before that teacher reaches the age of thirty. In a system with no credentials or qualifications, it's no wonder we ask, "Why is our newly appointed secretary of education not qualified for the position?"

The Courage to Change

Why do we all sit back and do nothing to stop the insanity in our public schools? We the people have the power to change policy by casting our votes and using our collective courage to band together and create the change we want to see. I believe we can make this happen.

- **What is it going to take** in our country, in our states, and in our communities to have the courage to stand up and say we want this current system to change? When will we say "Enough is enough" and come together to take action and make the needed changes? Will it be when we reach total privatization of schools so that each individual group, whether cultural, religious, or radical, can decide to teach what they want students to know in "their" corporate charter schools? Will we allow science to eliminate climate change, or will there be no science? Will we allow the history of our great country to be rewritten or erased so there is no evidence of the Holocaust or of slavery? Will we allow creative arts to disappear, the banning of books, and forbid entry of children who immigrate from other countries until they speak English? Will we allow computers and virtual instruction funded by big business to replace human teachers and allow wealthy politicians to dictate and mandate educational policy that puts more money in their pockets and does nothing for the educational development of our children? We are allowing these things to happen as we speak! Yes, not everyone believes in climate change, and virtual education has its place for students who are homebound or prefer online learning, but our forefathers created public schools to promote the greater good for all the people in our country and to eliminate an elitist system of education. George Orwell's *1984* could actually happen in 2024, if not sooner!

- **We the people** of the United States of America have the freedom, the right, and the power to stand up and demand a change in the direction our public schools are headed. Will we act before it is too late? In 2001, Dr. Phillip Schlechty's epilogue in *Shaking Up the Schoolhouse* gives a visionary report on the future of public schools in the year 2020. It is very close to what is happening in our world today. For example, he predicts small school cooperatives that control what their children learn based on their beliefs. He also predicts the use of vouchers to pull money away from public schools to fund for-profit charter schools, leaving public schools severely underfunded. School accountability is predicted to be totally controlled by the state, including the appointment of superintendents and school boards by state government officials instead of being elected or appointed at the local level.

His solution is a call to action for educational leaders to change the conditions making it impossible to restructure and systemically change schools and school systems. His prescience and doctoral background in the sociology of education has had a profound impact on my continued work in the quest for quality public education for all students.

- **Disruptive innovation:** In his book *The Innovator's Dilemma*, author Clayton Christensen distinguishes between two types of innovations—those that are sustaining and those that are disruptive. He explains that sustaining innovations are intended to improve effectiveness and efficiency and make it possible for the present system to perform up to capacity. Disruptive innovations call upon the system and those who work in it to do things they have never done. Sustaining innovations are neither more nor less than extensions of the present system and have little impact on either the structure or the culture of the system. Disruptive innovations, if they are to be employed effectively, require dramatic alteration in both the structure and the culture of the organization. Reformation versus transformation is an example of this dilemma. School reform is a sustaining innovation because its design is to improve the effectiveness and efficiency of the current education system. *Re-form* is "to form again." In other words, if you do what you've always done, you'll get what you've always got. Transformation in education is a disruptive innovation because it requires dramatic change in the structure and culture of the organization. In 2006, Phil Schlechty borrowed Clayton's ideas on the concept of disruptive innovation to illustrate what must be done to transform the structure and culture of public schools to invite innovation rather than implement mandates. In Schlechty's *Creating Great Schools: Six Critical Systems at the Heart of Educational Innovation,* he organizes his thinking around six social systems: recruitment; knowledge transmission; power and authority; evaluation; directional systems; and boundary systems and recommends the use of his systemic thinking for leaders and school communities to study their systems before recommending transformative change.

So, do we innovate or disintegrate? That is the question. I believe if we use disruptive innovations and change the culture and structure of public schools as I have illustrated through the wisdom of several educational-thought leaders, we can transform the way public schools do their "core business." Let's review what we can control and what must change in public schools:

* As educators, we can design and invent meaningful, intellectually demanding knowledge work for all students, work that authentically engages students in lifetime learning.
* As school leaders, we can create a climate and culture that's a motivational, innovative learning environment.
* As school communities, we can build positive relationships and engage everyone within our increasingly diverse populations.
* Public school systems must change by putting students at the top of the organizational chart and make their success and well-being the focus of all decisions.
* Local leaders must demand change at the state and national levels for our public school systems. We must stop the testing-versus-teaching dilemma and bring decision-making back to the teachers and district leaders who have the knowledge and expertise in regard to how students learn.
* Public school systems must change by pushing back against unfunded state mandates, informing their electorates to vote with their feet, and joining together across the states and country to stop the disintegration of democratic principles.
* **I believe we can "take back our public schools" one community at a time.** In the next three chapters, I will show how this is possible.

Relationships

"The meeting of two personalities is like the contact of two chemical substances: if there is any reaction, both are transformed."
—*Carl Gustav Jung*

Engaging Communities in Public Education

It is imperative that we engage everyone in our internal and external school communities in the education of our students. Our students are the future citizens, workers, leaders, and future caretakers of our neighborhoods, cities, states, country, and world! We have the power to shape their futures, to guide them, to coach them, and to mentor them with our collective wisdom for the greater good. We must allow people into our schools to see what incredible work is being done by our students and teachers. We must connect our students and their learning to the real world of work in our communities. This is the way we'll restore trust in public education.

In this chapter, I will show you how to market your school, create positive publicity, and make meaningful connections with outside groups, businesses, and organizations, then sit back and watch the magic happen!

Be Inviting—Just Ask!

- **How do you get people from outside your school and community to come see the innovations taking place at your school?** Why, you ask them! Invite everyone in the community and beyond to be a part of the educational process. There are many who would offer their talents and expertise at your school but feel intimidated or do not know how to get involved. Make a phone call, or have your students send handwritten notes. Invite the parents and families of the students. Invite local businesses and your local government. Stop in and give them an invitation face-to-face and a flyer to post where the public can see it. Invite school neighbors and retirees who may not have children in the school but who can become positive promoters or surrogate grandparents for your students. Send flyers or post them in high-traffic areas of the community, such as the library, the pharmacy, or the grocery store. Everyone who comes into the school provides an affirmation of the performance of our students. Just think of the motivation and pride students will feel in sharing their quality work with others beyond their teachers, peers, and principal. Imagine the delight of the student whose social studies project is affirmed by the mayor, or the kindergarten student whose artwork is selected to hang in a local business or organization!

- **Ask for volunteers** to serve throughout the year. Hold a volunteer coffee or tea in your cafeteria or media center and give attendees an overview of what they can do to assist you and your students. Have clipboards and sign-up sheets for them to choose activities tailored to their time and talents. Follow that with a tour of your school so they can see, hear, and feel the excitement of teaching and learning throughout the school. Have computers set up so that potential volunteers can complete the online application necessary for your district's security clearance. Then, before the end of the school year, have a special event to recognize and thank your volunteers. Involve students in the program and give the volunteers a certificate or a small token of appreciation. We held our volunteer appreciation during the week of Valentine's Day!

- **Invite local preschools** who will be sending incoming kindergarteners to your school. Have them bring their students on a field trip or give them an invitation to send home with their students for a special time when both parents and teachers can visit. Our schools also held a "Kindergarten Round-Up" each spring and advertised it in local newspapers, on our website, and with flyers sent home with the students. These could be shared with new families in the neighborhood. Set up a designated day during the last few weeks of school to hold tours so that families can come during these times or make an appointment for a school tour. At our school, this personalized customer service went a long way toward building relationships with each family and introducing each student to the WOW elementary school they were about to experience!

Positive Publicity

So much of the publicity the media shares about schools is negative and usually related to a sensational headline regarding bullying, a safety issue, or a parent complaint about a school policy or an employee. Why not be proactive and create some positive publicity? Be ready with a weekly press release for an upcoming event, such as new kindergartener orientation or an innovative learning activity where students build robots or learn how to code and create their own video games or apps.

- **Get to know your local newspaper reporters, and radio and TV stations** to create positive publicity for your school. Send out regular press releases for upcoming meetings and events to advertise to the public. Make sure the media has access to your school's website calendar so that if it is a slow news day for them, they may want to cover something happening at your school. Invite them to attend unique events at your school. Send pictures and prewritten articles that will pique their interest to come visit your school. Students should have signed media releases on file at the school for permission to use their photographs for public view.
- **Have an emergency publicity plan in place** so that if something happens that is not so positive, there is only one spokesperson to the press on behalf of the school. Make sure reporters do not

interview or take pictures of your students on school grounds without their parents' and your permission. Media should not interrupt the regular school day and should be escorted at all times when on campus. If you take the time to build positive relationships with media contacts, they will respect your boundaries and call on you if they are looking for information on a current topic.

Marketing Your School

With the increasing number of "free" charter schools popping up on neighborhood corners, and with the state and national push to provide parents with more choices for their children's education, it is becoming a necessity to market your public school. My schools were a part of the sixth largest school system in the nation, so I could not rely on my school district to market my individual school. In chapter 3, I talked about creating multiage classrooms and a school-within-a-school concept to attract families and give them choices within our school. In chapter 8, I will share how we created an innovative program to bring students back from private and charter schools and give parents another choice within our school. By creating an innovative district program, we also received additional marketing assistance from our district, which provided glossy brochures and recognition on the district website as a school choice for parents.

- **Make sure you have a logo with your mascot and school colors to brand your school.** The mascot we voted in during those first organizational meetings was a panther. The Florida panther is a protected species in our state. Each year the panther would appear dressed in theme for all our promotional materials.

    Share your vision, mission statement, values, and beliefs so that everyone knows your expectations and what makes your school unique to your way of doing business. Design and create a website that is updated weekly and gives essential information to students, parents, and the community at large. Use other forms of social media, such as Twitter, to stay connected with your followers and to send reminders. An automated call or text system is critical in handling emergencies or information that needs to get out to families quickly.

- **Send home a weekly newsletter and post it on your website.** Include up-to-date information on deadlines for field trips or school pictures and special calendar events. Adding student work and recognitions also generates interest. One of our extremely talented and creative teachers designed and produced a school newsletter that gave students affirmation for their quality work. Create a student handbook with information critical for parents. Ours was a glossy trifold folder we updated yearly to include changes in our school map or lunch prices.

  I created a media packet for parents after attending a Disney Institute class called "Marketing Your School." Before school started, we used it to hold registration forms and the various documents needed to enroll students in school. At the beginning of the year, we sent it home as a welcome back for families with a bumper sticker or calendar magnet, a grade-level school-supplies list, and flyers on how to join the PTA, become involved in the School Advisory Council, or volunteer at the school. Be sure to include a school calendar for the year and then update that calendar monthly in your newsletters and on your website. I also hired an approved vendor through my school-board purchasing department to update logos to yearly themes, print certificates and materials, and order rewards and incentives for students to keep the excitement and anticipation going all year long.

Communication Is Key

The key to effective communication is to use as many venues as possible to reach the greatest amount of individuals. Some people like to communicate through written announcements, while others like auditory messages. Those with vision or hearing problems may communicate better face-to-face. Of course, email, texting, and Twitter have become more popular in later years with pocket technology and busy schedules.

- **Communicate, communicate, communicate!** Use as many ways as you can to reach all styles of learning and processing. You can use visual communication through newsletters, flyers, posters, school marquees, banners, websites, high-traffic community locations, newspapers, and local publications. Auditory communication can come in the form of daily announcements on the school morning TV show, afternoon intercom reminders, local radio and television stations, or voice and video messages on your website.

  Communication should be personal and face-to-face as much as possible! Being visible during arrival and dismissal times in the carpool lane is one way to have personal contact with students, staff, and parents on a regular basis. Chatting with students during lunch periods in the cafeteria is a way to keep a pulse on what students are thinking, saying, and how they are feeling about school and about themselves. Being visually present during the school day also allows you to give compliments and to catch them doing good.

- **Internal communication is also critical.** Calendars, flyers, posters, emails, reminders, announcements, and a daily notice board are all excellent ways to keep the information flowing. As I shared earlier, the more correct information you share up front with everyone, the less incorrect information and rumors you must deal with later. Remember, if information is power, then *you* have "the power to empower" others by sharing the correct information in a transparent way. You should reserve scheduled internal staff meetings for professional development opportunities, decision-making issues, or questions and answers on "burning issues." You can communicate regular business announcements through email or the other previously mentioned venues. That way you send a strong message that you value everyone's time.

  Our new school had a population of over one thousand students, and our teachers and staff were all new to the facility and to each other. One day, I held a "Who Moved My Cheese" (see Dr. Spencer Johnson, author) party after school with sparkling cider and cheese bites so we could all "whine" about how we could get to know each other better. I even borrowed a "cheese head" from a Green Bay Packers fan to wear on my head. *Who Moved My Cheese: An Amazing Way to Deal with Change in Your Work and Your Life* was a popular business fable about two mice finding their cheese, or happiness, in a new environment. This reflected our new school situation perfectly. Having a sense of humor and a big smile always made everything better. This led to our theme for our second year, "High Five, Keep the Dream Alive," which was based on Ken Blanchard's new book, *High Five: The Magic of Working Together*. We started that year off with a scavenger hunt for teachers to discover what was upstairs, downstairs, and around each corner of our school.

- **Ask for feedback from all leadership groups** and continuously monitor quality results. For example, ask, "How are we doing?" "Is this working for you?" "Do you have any suggestions about . . . ?" "How can we do better with . . . ?" Our regularly scheduled leadership team meetings included a formal agenda but allowed a brief time for questions and feedback. We used the same format with our School Advisory Council meetings, which included representation from all shareholder groups and allowed time for questions and feedback at the end of monthly meetings. We had some of the best conversations and ideas come from these meetings because we created a safe, risk-free environment where everyone felt comfortable communicating openly and honestly.

Making Connections

In chapter 3, I shared a few examples of the importance of making connections for students across curriculum areas to reinforce concepts and solidify learning. In chapters 4 and 5, we talked about the power of building positive relationships and making connections with people both internally and externally in the school community and beyond. Here are some other great ideas and ways my schools made connections for students through curriculum; our neighborhood; school district; local, state, and federal governments; across the country with other schools; and even with a university on the other side of the world!

- **Our entrepreneurial school model allowed us more autonomy** with choice of curriculum materials for students. Instead of buying a textbook program, we based our reading program on *Mosaic of Thought: Teaching Comprehension in a Readers Workshop Approach.* Our teachers met regularly with our reading coach to refine and practice comprehension strategies. We had an extensive reading resource room with real books—big books, little books, and chapter books for all levels of readers—which teachers would check out for groups of students to learn and practice comprehension strategies. One of the strategies taught was "making connections." Students learned three kinds of connections to make while reading the text: text to self, text to text, and text to world. As students spoke and wrote about these types of connections, teachers could evaluate each student's level of reasoning and understanding and intervene as necessary. We adopted these same strategies to make sense of the connections we made with our community members—connection to school, connection to each other, and connection to the world.

- **Connections with parents and extended families** of students were the most important, but getting families to engage with us on behalf of their students was always a challenge. Parent-teacher conferences were often difficult to hold because of work schedules. Getting parents to connect with other parents during evening activities was sometimes easier if it was after their workday and we provided childcare for other siblings. Food was always a benefit, and the PTA sometimes made pizza preorders available so families would not have to worry about dinner. Connecting parents and students to the world was also something we could do with our state-of-the-art technology and resources.

- **Connections with local government and community resources** became increasingly important as families became more in need of those services. Our cafeteria manager was phenomenal when it came to connecting families and community resources. Because the city had donated the land to the school board for our school, we had a reciprocal agreement that they could use our facility for community meetings and vice versa. The city's Parks and Recreation Department also used our facility for a summer camp for students, which our families took advantage of during their workday. The medical center, police and fire departments, sports park, pool, and performing arts center were all within walking distance of our school. City officials had monthly meetings with principals and parent groups to keep the lines of communication open and offered services and activities to us. We also kept them informed of school activities and the services our staff and students could offer them.

- **Local businesses, craftsmen, and artisans** have talents you can tap into to provide for your school needs, and, in turn, you can give them exposure and increased business by acknowledging and recognizing their work in your school community.

  In December of our first year, we held a formal dedication ceremony with the superintendent of schools, school-board members, and city leaders officially cutting the ribbon and declaring us open and operational. We held it on our school basketball courts on a mobile stage the city had loaned us. Our very own district Art Teacher of the Year directed the creation of an awesome student-produced set, decorations, and the artwork and floral arrangements for the reception. A high-school horticulture class transported and set up the plants gracing the stage. Our sixth-grade teacher and students coordinated and buried a PVC-pipe time capsule to be unearthed ten years later. Our "Singing Stars" entertained us, and our entire student body dressed in primary colors and strategically formed a rainbow as the audience behind the VIP section. This rainbow was another metaphor illustrating the beautiful diversity of our children! A third-grade student sang the "Star-Spangled Banner" solo and blew everyone away as possibly the next Brittney Spears! One of our parent-leaders arranged for a helicopter to fly overhead and video the entire event. A parent came forward with his video company and offered to professionally record and make videotapes parents could buy, and another parent with a printing business made our invitations and programs. The cover design, of course, was a fourth-grade student's creation, again reinforcing the core business of our learning organization. It took a whole page in that program to recognize all our partners in education for their contributions and labors of love for this memorable event!

- **Retirement communities or homes** can provide historical and meaningful relationships for students whose grandparents may not live nearby. A few of our classes often visited one of these assisted-living homes, where they sang songs at holiday times and shared handmade projects with the residents, brightening their day. It gave the students a sense of purpose. Retirees who were able to come to our school loved to read to the students or help in the classrooms for a brief period of time. It was especially heartwarming to see the connections made between the students who had immigrated from other countries and retirees whose roots were from those same countries and who spoke the same language.

- **Connections with school-board members and district resources** are always helpful, as I have outlined in past chapters, in initiating and moving construction or safety projects along, or in providing "outside expertise" to teach or reinforce a new program you are wanting to implement at your school. Connections with other schools in your feeder pattern (innovation zone) can also create greater continuity for students, parents, and families, pre-K–12. Our zone facilitator, or lead principal, created a partnership program that gathered parent, business, and community partners from all of our schools on a monthly basis to share ideas and resources, and present a continuity of services.

- **Connections with state and national legislators** available through the state and federal governments and organizations can also be valuable resources, of which I have given several examples. Those making the decisions at these levels must have firsthand experiences upon which to base their research and votes. Sending parent- and teacher-leaders to our state capital during legislative sessions or visiting their local offices during the off-season keeps these connections alive and in the forefront of their thinking.

- **Our connections with a principal's academy group from the Schlechty Center** led to the honor of hosting a follow-up mini conference of principals from around the country at our WOW school. They spent two days with us learning from all our amazing students and teachers and visiting classrooms to see "Working on the Work" in action. This opportunity elevated the quality of the work teachers provided to students and the work students provided their teachers. In other words, it was a *national* affirmation for others to visit and have such high regard for our teaching and learning model.

- **Our global connections and a Japanese university delegation visit** to our school was one of the ultimate highlights of being able to make that "us to the real world" connection for our students and ourselves. This came about through a conference I attended in 1996, the Annual Conversation of the International Network of Principals' Centers. I belonged to our local South Florida Center for Educational Leaders, and we were hosting this international conference that year, with more than eighteen countries in attendance. It was there that my assistant principal and I met a Japanese university professor studying school leadership in the United States. A dozen years later, I receive a call informing me that he and a delegation from his university were coming to Florida again and would like to arrange a visit to our school on their tour. What a thrill for our staff and students to meet them, share our daily work for achieving quality, and exchange student-made artifacts they would remember and treasure for years to come!

Where Magic Happens

Remember the spectacular "Building Dreams" dedication ceremony we held our first year? I would also like to paint a picture of other events and themes we created at our WOW School of the Century. Here are some of those pictures of practice:

- **"Dreams Take Flight"—Up, Up, and Away Day** was one of my favorites. That year we focused on taking flight, and we found a hot-air balloonist who came to our schools and did an inside/outside demonstration of hot-air balloon flight. Early in the morning in the spring, after our final bell rang for school to begin, we called all classes to meet outside on the basketball courts again to see the balloon unfolded on the ground. With a microphone and sound system, the balloonist shared his story of the practical scientific principles of successful balloon flights, the importance of the right weather conditions, and the skills needed by the pilot to make it all happen. Right before their eyes, the balloon inflated as the red flames blasted into its center, and if it hadn't been tethered to the ground, it would have taken off right then and there! WOW! When students went back to their classrooms, the balloon was moved into the cafeteria, unfolded, and again groups of students were called to come and sit inside the balloon as more stories of science and flight were told! We scheduled this the day before our high-stakes state testing as a reward for the students' demanding work and preparation and to motivate them to "fly high" with knowledge and confidence on the tests in the days ahead.

  We opened that year with a welcome-back trip for teachers and staff to the "Butterfly Capital of the World," which was in a

neighboring city just a few miles away. We toured the attraction and bought chrysalises to take back to our classrooms, but before we returned, we had a cookout and picnic lunch at a park and talked about a phenomenon in chaos theory and weather prediction called "the butterfly effect." This scientific concept purports that when a butterfly flaps its wings in Brazil, for example, a tornado can be set off in Texas, or, in quantum physics theory, small changes in the system can create a ripple effect that causes greater results. With generous donations from a prominent South Florida developer and environmentalist, we also created a butterfly garden that year. On Teacher/Staff Appreciation Day, we held a school-wide butterfly release with all students present!

We also watched clips from a movie called *October Sky*, which is based on the book *Rocket Boys*—the true story of four boys living in a coal-miner's town in West Virginia who become inspired by the launching of *Sputnik* in 1957. Through the wisdom and innovation of their teacher, who launches them into learning rocketry, they win the National Science Fair. The boy who attends wins first prize, receives many offers for college scholarships, and eventually becomes a NASA engineer. As a follow-up, teachers launched paper rockets with their students to demonstrate motion, velocity, acceleration, distance, and time. This was the year STEM (science, technology, engineering, and mathematics) education became a priority around the country.

- **"Reel Dreams"—Dancing Under the Stars Community Block Party** evolved from a suggestion from a group of teacher-leaders brainstorming ideas to increase parent and community involvement at school. "Why not have a block party to bring everyone together for a night of fun like we do in our neighborhoods?" they asked. Inviting residents to a nonthreatening activity just might be the answer, they believed. The fun began right then and there! One balmy night in early November, we found ourselves on our school's basketball courts again, with that same mobile stage borrowed from the city. Each grade level of teachers had prepared a variety of dances they would teach to the audience, who would then join in and interact with them. Our art club again designed and created the stage décor and surrounding areas to reflect the popular *Dancing with the Stars* TV show. They also presented an incredible art exhibition. We had a new, enthusiastic music teacher that year who had totally engaged the kids in singing, dancing, playing the keyboard and violins, and there was even a drum line! WOW! Over five hundred families, students, staff, and community members attended, enjoying the music, dancing, food, and friendship throughout the evening. Local businesses, organizations, and vendors surrounded the dance area. A parent who is a professional DJ arranged the backup music, and there was even a surprise visit by the Miami HEAT Dancers! The show's finale was the entire fifth-grade team of teachers and students leading everyone in "I Gotta Feeling" by the Black-Eyed Peas. It's funny how music and dance can bring people together in such a powerful way. Talk about authentic engagement!

- **"Celebrate the Rhythm of the World"** showcased the importance of students and the arts. You would think we would have had enough of planning and preparing for major events, but the truth of the matter was, we were just getting warmed up. In early April of this same school year, every student had the opportunity to perform live, on a real stage, at our city's performing arts center, located right across the street from our school. It was an extravaganza of multicultural arts, music, and movement. Our respected, admired, and talented reading specialist was our master of ceremonies, fashionably rocking her authentic African dress and head wrap. We sold over 1,400 seats that night. Each grade level of students sang; some student soloists played the piano, guitar, and drums; and we were entertained by the strings club, chorus, and our now-famous drum line. The finale was our chorus members singing "We Are the World" and then asking everyone to join in. This event was a statement to the community about the importance of not cutting the arts at elementary schools as our district was facing a $130 million shortfall from the state.

- **"A Decade of Dreams," our ten-year anniversary community celebration,** took place in November 2010. It was hard to believe ten years of Working on the Work for quality results had gone by. It took a village to prepare for this important milestone and to reconnect with ten years of relationships from our past and present. It began with an invitation that had a cover designed by one of our outstanding students with autism. He was recognized and presented with a plaque featuring his design and a duplicate that would remain permanently at our school. The local Civil Air Patrol Color Guard presented the colors, and two students led us in the Pledge of Allegiance. The absolute coolest part of the program was the same student, now attending a state university majoring in theatre and music production (remember the next Brittney Spears?), returning to sing the "Star-Spangled Banner" ten years later! State representatives, school-board members, the mayor, and city commissioners brought greetings and remarks, and the mayor presented us with a citywide proclamation for our "Decade of Dreams."

  By now I'm sure you can picture us all on our school basketball court with the same stage but with different creative décor, of course, and students from chorus, drum-line and strings clubs performing for the crowd. One of the most special moments was the dedication of a memorial tree for two of our most beloved teachers and staff members who had passed away. Sixty-four vendors set up tables, booths, and food trucks, and a talented local high school senior and videographer recorded our event this time. Over one hundred student alumni and their families returned to dig up and open the time capsule we'd buried during our dedication. The looks on their faces when they found their work and artifacts from the year 2000 in that time capsule were priceless! Individuals and families could also purchase ceramic tiles to paint and decorate, which would later be fired in a kiln and permanently placed on a legacy wall, which still preserves those memories for years to come.

- **"Passport to Your Dreams"—A Multicultural Exhibition** was our grandest exhibition of the students' quality work and one I was most proud of. It was May 2012, and we were ending a year of studying continents, countries, and cultures school-wide. Each grade-level hallway chose a continent, and each classroom a country within that continent. Students in each classroom designed their country's flag out of their choice of recycled materials. During International Peace Day, our art club magically "grew" a giant "peace tree," with branches reaching far and wide, displaying messages of peace from every student in our school. Those creations remained displayed in our main hallway the entire year. The multicultural exhibition took place on a Saturday, and everyone who attended received a passport they could have stamped as they traveled around our world of continents and countries. African masks, the Great Barrier Reef, Monet's Garden, the Great Wall of China, a live Black history wax museum, a museum of science and history, hands-on science labs, multimedia presentations, portfolio sharing, 3-D Florida tourism, Greek mythology, the Leaning Tower of *Pizza* (constructed with pizza boxes), and Mexican crafts were just a few of the totally student-produced products on display. South American sambas, Waltzing Matildas, and a production of songs from seven continents could be heard, along with the excited chatter of students sharing their work products with our guests. Many school district officials attended, as well as city and community dignitaries. Even local artists affiliated with the city art museum came and marveled over a Chinese dragon as long as a hallway! Multicultural foods were also available, and our annual PTA carnival rounded out the day. This was truly a representation of our community and a perfect example of engaging students, parents, and the community at large in meaningful, authentic quality work.

- **Our Polar Express Day** was a much smaller experience but one that became annual and was near and dear to my heart. Our assistant principal was dressed in authentic costume as the conductor, and our cafeteria manager and her team served up the "Hot, hot, hot" chocolate for everyone, along with some volunteer elves who helped with the pouring. All our students and staff would wear their most comfortable pajamas for the day and read the story while the movie and music ran all day long during the students' lunch periods in the cafeteria. My office manager/confidential secretary who joined me in 2005 skillfully coordinated the day's activities (as she did on a daily basis) and was especially proud of making it snow on this day every year! She would search high and low for the "snow juice" for our snow machine and then supervise the facilities staff for its perfect placement at the top of our covered walkway. As the students exited the cafeteria after lunch, the snow would begin to fall, and the delight on the face of every child, ages four to thirty-nine, was something to behold and treasure forever. At the end of the day, everyone received a silver sleigh bell to remind them to always BELIEVE. Because that was what we were all about as a school and a learning community—believing in ourselves and in each other and never giving up on our dreams, no matter how big or small.

Relationships

"You can make more friends in two months by becoming interested in other people than you can in two years by trying to get other people interested in you."

—*Dale Carnegie*

Testing versus Teaching: Killing the Joy of Learning

As you can see from my experiences as an elementary principal for the twenty-two years of my thirty-plus years in public education, there was a progressive move from teaching the "whole child" academically, developmentally, socially, and emotionally, to teaching to a state test. This test assessed each child's yearlong body of work through reading, writing, or computing and neatly bubbling in answers on an answer sheet. In addition to the big test, there were also district tests the students were required to take on a regular basis to prepare for the big test.

Eventually, teachers found themselves spending all their time testing, with less and less time for teaching for understanding, deep and thought-provoking teaching, or teaching that authentically engaged and encouraged students to be excited and persistent in their learning. Don't get me wrong—teachers do not mind being accountable *for* learning requirements for standards in their content areas or the context of the age group of students they teach. They have always been measured by their students' success, but they used to be able to personalize instruction for each child and focus on that child's individual strengths when deciding how they would demonstrate mastery of their learning. What they do mind is being accountable *to* state legislators, politicians, and for-profit corporations that create laws, tests, and evaluation systems as unfunded mandates that promote big business in education. The tests require a "one size fits all" approach to student learning and have replaced the opportunity for profound learning in the classroom. This testing culture is still found in my state and across the nation today.

Despite the relentless focus on testing, there are some positive moves to provide hands-on, minds-on activities in the areas of science, technology, engineering, and mathematics (STEM). However, this is a direct contradiction of the testing culture, so how do teachers find time to do it all? Their preference would be the STEM activities, but their evaluations and paychecks are based on "the test."

STEM: Science, Technology, Engineering, and Mathematics

When the acronym STEM was first introduced by the National Science Foundation in 2001, there was a growing concern that the United States was lagging behind other countries in science, technology, engineering, and mathematics and was not preparing a sufficient number of students, teachers, and professionals in those areas. Due to an aging workforce, our country also needed more specialists in these fields to compete in an innovative global marketplace. In other words, we were not preparing our young people for the jobs that did not currently exist. A common definition is as follows: *"STEM education is an interdisciplinary approach to learning where rigorous academic concepts are coupled with real-world lessons as students apply science, technology, engineering, and mathematics in contexts that make connections between school, community, work, and the global enterprise enabling the development of STEM literacy and with it the ability to compete in the STEM new economy"* (Tsupros, 2009).

In 2006, President George W. Bush announced the American Competitive Initiative in his State of the Union address, and later, President Obama signed into law the STEM Education Act of 2015. These provided a strong future of workforce development and education in these scientific areas.

- **Principal Promise Program—A Florida STEM initiative**
  In December 2009, I was one of fifty elementary-school principals initially involved in the state Principal PROMiSE (Partnership to Rejuvenate and Optimize Mathematics and Science Education in Florida) Program at Florida State University's Learning Systems Institute. This yearlong program gave me the opportunity to select a rising-star fifth-grade teacher-leader to join with me and other colleagues throughout the state to bring back and share the knowledge we'd gleaned with other the teachers in our school and district. This rising star became an intern and assistant principal soon after and is currently a practicing innovative principal in the district.

- **A K–5 hands-on science lab program** was a STEM initiative we created at our school to give students a hands-on, minds-on lab experience to follow up the science instruction they received in their classrooms. I selected another fifth-grade teacher-leader who was extremely passionate about science education to create an authentic learning environment for students and to teach in the lab, integrating the sciences with other curriculum areas.

- **A K–5 hands-on technology lab** existed at our school, and classroom teachers took their students there so everyone would have individual access to a computer. I selected a teacher-assistant who was very knowledgeable in technology and had a flair for creativity to work with teachers on project-based learning activities that integrated technology with the other sciences and curriculum areas.

- **Hands-on mathematics and engineering concepts** became more prevalent at our school as additional teachers began to team up to design lessons and engage their students in projects that included simple machines, the kinetic energy of motion, robotics, and the physics of roller coasters. Out of these projects came an idea from two highly effective and innovative teachers to develop a project-based learning opportunity I will explain in detail later in this chapter.

The Importance of the Arts

An unfortunate number of schools have sacrificed their art or music programs to fund additional staff to reteach lagging learners on the necessary remediation to improve their scores on "the test." Many students are motivated to come to school because of participation in an arts program and being able to express themselves and their gifts through the visual arts or by playing violin, piano, drums, or singing in chorus. So again, in direct contradiction with the testing focus, a great national debate begins as to whether the arts should be added to STEM to make it STEAM. No, folks, I am not making this up!

It's a wonderful debate to have—whether or not we should add creative thinking to critical thinking and broaden our students' horizons. But guess what? Our students are not allowed think critically or creatively in authentic learning scenarios because they are too busy making sure they do not "draw outside the bubbles on *the test*."

- **STEM or STEAM?** The great debate began shortly after the STEM movement, when teachers of the arts began to say, "What about us and the arts? Are we going to be replaced by all the educational dollars focused on the sciences? Can't we add the A to STEM and become STEAM?" So the art of creative thinking and the design process were added, and today the promoters of STEAM are saying, "Rather than focus on rote memorization or mastery of separate topics, STEAM uses project-based teaching to holistically foster students' skills in creativity, design thinking, tech literacy, collaboration, and problem-solving. This sets students up for *success* in STEM, especially those who might not seem to be naturally gifted in technical areas" (www.stemtosteam.org).

    All of this takes us back to the success I have seen using the Working on the Work framework. Designing and creating intellectually demanding knowledge work for students is critical to their level of authentic engagement when learning content areas that are difficult. What is difficult for one student may not be difficult for another, thus the concept of creating collaborative learning teams to focus on the strengths of each individual and to use both critical and creative thinking to solve real-world problems—this is design thinking, innovation, and quality teaching and learning at its best!

- **Creative thinking and budgeting** to keep our arts and music programs was a challenge in 2010 when our district faced the $130 million shortfall of funding in the state of Florida. Our parents and community were very supportive of our commitment because they had seen the results through the eyes of our students. Attendance was up, discipline issues were down, and there was an increase in the artistic abilities and self-confidence of our students.

  Our School Advisory Council concurred with our budget recommendations when we decided to get rid of our librarian position, cut down on materials and supplies, and not replace a teacher's aide. We had a highly competent media clerk who knew our inventory inside and out, and we no longer needed media as a special class. Teachers scheduled class time to check out books, and our technology lab replaced library time. Some of our materials and supplies were redundant and, with the increase of computers and laptops, no longer served a purpose. We also kept the School Advisory Council informed on school operations and were always transparent with our budget and the decisions we had to make.

- **Becoming a Title I school** also factored into the decisions we made with prioritizing our arts programs. Title I is a federally funded program that gives financial aid to schools with high numbers of low-income students to ensure that all students can meet challenging academic standards. Our poverty rate had grown to over 60 percent. Parents and families no longer had the money or the time to provide their children with enrichment activities such as the arts or athletics outside of the school setting. Title I also mandated an increase in parent involvement, so what better way to get parents involved than to invite them to watch their students perform free of charge!

Physical Education and Movement

Former First Lady Michelle Obama's mission and passion was a program called "Let's Move." Its purpose was to encourage America's children and families to live healthier lives through physical activity and nutritional eating. Physical education became a mandate in many states, but there was no funding to support PE teachers. Therefore, teachers were again faced with another dilemma—include physical education in their classroom routines to meet the states' unfunded mandate, or teach to the test that would decide their evaluation score and paycheck? "How can we fit it all in?" they cried.

- **Formal physical education programs** are critical to the health and well-being of our students. We provided a full-time physical education program in prekindergarten through fifth grade with a highly certified and skilled physical education teacher and coach. His certifications also included those for students with special needs and early childhood education. In 2009, Florida passed legislation that elementary students must have 150 minutes of physical education per week or no less than thirty consecutive minutes on any day it takes place.

- **Dance, yoga, and mindfulness** were also a part of our social/emotional learning activities to help students relax, focus, and practice empathy and kindness. One of my favorite examples was a most energetic and upbeat master teacher who regularly used yoga in her classroom to reduce anxiety, especially before testing. Our superintendent of schools came out for a visit and happened upon one of these yoga sessions in this third-grade classroom. He immediately engaged with the students and was excited to see their positive reaction to his willing participation.

- **Physical arrangement of classroom configurations** is important for movement of students throughout the school day. Some students need to move more often than others, and some learn most effectively standing, sitting on the floor, or kneeling at a shorter table. Flexible classroom setups give students a choice of what kind of learning space works best for them. Traditional settings, like rows of perfectly placed desks, do not lend themselves to collaboration, communication, and engagement with curriculum and other students.

- **Special activities such as Jump Rope for Heart, Field Day, and Miami Dolphins Day** added other interests and excitement to the physical education program. Jump Rope for Heart is a thirty-five-year national initiative of the American Heart Association. Students learned jump rope skills to take care of their hearts while experiencing the good feeling of raising money to give back to the community. Field Day was a half-day or day-long event with games appropriate to grade level, where students could practice teamwork and sportsmanship and just have fun! We were fortunate to live twenty miles north of the Miami Dolphins training facility and took advantage of a simulation training camp they offered on-site at our school.

- **The after-school-care program activities** of our award-winning program were an extension of our learning during the regular school day. It was important to us that we had continuity using school personnel the students already knew and with whom they felt comfortable. Students were able to complete their homework with professional assistance and not have to take it home to do later in the evening. Additional physical education activities such as tae kwon do and cheerleading were also available in our after-school-care program, as well as art, music, technology, and the sciences. Students competed in reading and writing challenges and had opportunities for snack time, conversation, and interaction with their peers. Parents were pleased because their students were safe, happy, engaged, and learning!

Creativity and Innovation Abounds

Earlier in this chapter, I mentioned the two innovative teachers who created and developed a project-based learning opportunity that became a district Innovative Program. It started with our attendance at a gifted-learning symposium featuring Dr. Joseph Renzulli, professor of Educational Psychology at the University of Connecticut and director of the National Research Center on the Gifted and Talented. He and his wife, Dr. Sally Reis, are the founders of the Joseph S. Renzulli Gifted and Talented Academy in Hartford, Connecticut, and the Renzulli Creativity Program and Renzulli Learning System. They shared with us their life research focused on the identification and development of creativity and giftedness in young people and applying the strategies of gifted education to the improvement of learning for *all* students.

- **The belief that *all* children are gifted** in some area of their learning and that schools are places for talent development shaped the vision for our innovative program. The district was losing students to the new charter school movement and identified the need for alternative creative opportunities parents could choose for their children. We submitted our proposal, applied for grant funding, and decided it would reside in a new building that had been added to our school. We spent the remaining months of the school year planning curriculum delivery, identifying potential students, and marketing our innovative program to parents in and beyond our school community. We named it "Compass: A New Direction."

- **The Compass program** was a project-based learning opportunity that connected common core standards to real-world problem-solving and community partnerships. Students in the program had the opportunity to learn in multiage groupings and a technology-rich environment based on their interests. It began with students in grades K–3 and expanded as students moved up in their grade levels. Gifted students and students with special needs were included. The Compass classrooms used individual student iPads and tablets, interactive student whiteboards in every classroom, and distance learning partnerships. Their assessments were authentic and performance-based, including quarterly exhibitions of quality work products based on their thematic units of instruction. The first year, we brought forty-five additional students back to public school through Compass in addition to the students who were already enrolled at our school. The program was endorsed by both the Renzulli and Schlechty centers, and the parents loved it!

Returning the Joy to Learning

- **What do YOU remember about a special time at school when you were excited about learning?** Was it your performance in a play, a problem you solved, or a teacher who made a difference in your life? Did your family and community believe in you, encourage you, and cheer you on? Did you believe you could do anything you set your mind to? Did you look forward to working with your friends and classmates every day to solve a problem or invent something that would change the world? That is the joy of learning—working hard, achieving your goals and dreams, and having fun doing it!

- **Time spent on testing and preparation for testing is out of control.** Isn't it ironic that with all the wonderful opportunities our teachers have in our state and around the country for integrating curriculum content areas, using technology, and making connections for students, the greatest percent of teachers' time is spent on test preparation and teaching to and for the test? Each year I found it more difficult as a principal to protect my teachers from outside interests and forces and to give them time to teach for the best interests of the children.

- **Hands-on, minds-on learning is becoming extinct.** Now, teachers must teach the same scripted lesson in every class on every grade level, and someone from the district comes in to make sure that is happening. If not, the teacher and the principal are threatened with a "needs improvement" on their evaluations, which goes into a permanent record open to the public in some states. We know that children learn in different ways on different days, and yet teachers are required by state and district mandates to teach everyone in a cookie-cutter fashion. Schools receive letter grades from A to F based on the performance of their students on one state test. Teacher evaluations are based on the performance of students they did not even teach. What is wrong with this picture? Are our schools failing us, or are we failing our schools?

Are we going to continue to sit on our hands and watch this happen year after year, or are we going to answer the call to action and use our knowledge, expertise, and voices and say "Enough is enough!" We are now losing our third generation of critical and creative thinkers. Students are not prepared for the workplace because they do not have the experience of working in problem-solving teams or learning "soft skills," like writing a résumé or interviewing for a job, because there is no time for social-emotional learning to take place in a test-focused classroom! What is it going to take to get us back on our feet?

Relationships

"What students lack in school is an intellectual relationship or conversation with the teacher."
—William Glasser

Public Education: The Cornerstone of Our Democracy

Education for ALL students

What did the forefathers and political leaders of our democratic society think and say about public education? The first instance of tying the concept of public education to democracy was in the eighteenth century.

- **Thomas Jefferson** believed that enlightened citizens were necessary for the proper functioning of a republic. He said, "Above all things, I hope the education of the common people will be attended to. Convinced that on their good sense we may rely with the most security for the preservation of a due degree of Liberty," (Thomas Jefferson to James Madison, 1787, *On Politics and Government*, chapter 39.1: "Educating the People, No Freedom Without Education"). He also states, "A system of general instruction, which shall reach every description of our citizens from the richest to the poorest, as it was the earliest, so it will be the latest of all public concerns in which I shall permit myself to take an interest" (Thomas Jefferson to Joseph C. Cabell, 1818, *On Politics and Government,* chapter 39.4: "Educate Every Citizen").

  Thus was born the notion of educating the masses, or as we know it, public education.

- **Horace Mann** is considered the father of the Common School Movement. As the first secretary of education in the state of Massachusetts in 1837, he said, "The public school is the greatest discovery made by man. Education is best provided in schools embracing children of all religious, social and ethnic backgrounds." He was the first American education advocate to believe the people should be taxed to pay for, maintain, and control education. He also established normal schools for teacher preparation and training, which he thought was vital to public education ("The Horace Mann League of the USA," www.hmleague.org).

- **President Franklin D. Roosevelt** said, "Education is the cornerstone of a democratic society." He also observed that "democracy cannot succeed unless those who express their choice are prepared to choose wisely. The real safeguard of democracy, therefore, is education." Increasing levels of education, according to Roosevelt, "has given to this country a population more literate, more cultured, in the best sense of the word, more aware of the complexities of modern civilized life than ever before in our history." (The American Presidency Project: Franklin D. Roosevelt 124 - Message for Education Week September 27, 1938.)

The Law

- **"Public school" means any elementary or secondary institution operated by a state or governmental agency within the state** or operated through the use of governmental funds or property from that state or governmental agency. The public school system is administered by the federal Department of Education, but states are responsible for maintaining and operating public schools to comply with both state and federal laws. Education laws include attendance requirements; liability; curriculum standards; testing procedures; school finance; student financial aid; constitutional rights, like school prayer and student expression on school grounds; nondiscrimination; and school safety.

Students with Disabilities

- **Public law 94-142, or the Education for All Handicapped Children Act, was passed by the 94th Congress in 1975.** This law requires that all states who receive federal funding for students provide handicapped students with "a free and appropriate education within the least restrictive environment." That environment means students should be placed with nonhandicapped peers to the greatest extent appropriate. It also requires each student have an individualized educational plan (IEP), an appropriate evaluation, parent and teacher participation, and procedural safeguards that give parents due process to challenge placement decisions. In 1990, the United States Congress reauthorized the law and named it the Individuals with Disabilities Act (IDEA).

Productive Citizens

Let's look at some ways public education contributes to the preparation of productive citizens:

- **Citizenship** is another guiding principle of public education. "To prepare people to become responsible citizens; to improve social conditions; to promote cultural unity; to help people become economically self-sufficient; and to enhance individual happiness and enrich individual lives" was how the Center for Education Policy defined public education in a 1996 report. Being a U.S. citizen gives each person the right to vote, the right to serve on a jury and receive a fair trial by jury, freedom of speech, freedom of worship, and the freedom to pursue "life, liberty, and the pursuit of happiness," as stated in the Declaration of Independence. Citizenship gives everyone a voice but also comes with the responsibility to be an advocate of "the greater good" for our country and its people.

- **Service to your country and your community** are two other responsibilities of being a productive citizen. Participating in the democratic process, serving in the armed forces in defense of your country, obeying the laws of the land, and respecting the rights, opinions and beliefs of others are some of the ways we serve our community. In a school setting, teaching students to be good citizens and giving them opportunities to volunteer and participate in community activities helps them make connections between what they're learning and the real world. The community also benefits by supporting students in becoming contributing, civic-minded adults and future leaders and problem-solvers.

- **Future workforce preparation and readiness** can result from teaching, modeling, and exploring through actual experiences, even at the elementary-school level. When we talk about preparing students for the world of work, what do we mean? Do we ask what employers are looking for when hiring workers for twenty-first-century jobs? A strong work ethic, a positive attitude, communication skills, interpersonal skills, perseverance, teamwork, collaboration skills, critical thinking, and problem-solving are a few the Department of Labor defines as essential job skills. These are known as "soft-skills," or life skills, and do not look or sound like what we teach for the FCAT (Florida Comprehensive Assessment Tests) or other state-mandated assessments. An excellent resource is the Coalition of Adult Basic Education website (www.coabe.org), which includes vocational and technical careers and alternatives to the high-school-to-college pipeline, such as completing a high school education and receiving a general educational diploma (GED).

Two of the successes I have already mentioned were bringing in career speakers throughout the year and integrating them into our curriculum, not just on the formal "Career Day," and using technology to connect students to workers in other parts of the city, country, and world through distance learning or FaceTime. Another experience our fifth-grade students had for one full day each year was a local trip to Junior Achievement World: BizTown, a simulation city with eighteen different businesses and a wide range of "employment" opportunities. Junior Achievement USA is an active organization that reaches 4.4 million students in the United States and a total of 10.2 million students around the world. Their programs are delivered by more than two hundred thousand corporate and community volunteers who provide mentoring, internships, and financial literacy skills. An excellent reference is a blueprint they published in 2010: "Are Students Prepared for the Workplace?" (See www.juniorachievement.org)

Philanthropic Communities and Service Learning

Giving back to the community is an important lesson we modeled and taught the students at our school. It was a powerful way to show civic responsibility to our students and that giving to others less fortunate than ourselves is a gift in and of itself. It was also a way to engage students in an authentic, real-world experience and teach them empathy for others. We won our state's prestigious Five Star School Award for our many exceptional service-learning projects. I will share a story of one of those projects.

- **A Work of "Heart"** was a service-learning project initiated by our art teacher. It began in late August of 2005, after Hurricane Katrina passed through South Florida and ended up in the New Orleans area. Our art teacher was from a town near New Orleans, and her childhood home, still owned by her family, was destroyed by the hurricane. Our staff decided to "adopt" a school from the town where our art teacher grew up. Students in kindergarten through fifth grade art classes made New Orleans–themed ceramic pins and magnets out of clay and fired them in our kiln. Then they decorated them with paint, sequins, beads, feathers, and other items found in the art room. Even our staff participated in "art therapy" and decorated pins on a teacher planning day. The art club sold the pins for a dollar or two before school in the morning, at PTA meetings, and at other school functions.

    We also collected donations of books, crayons, and other school supplies the New Orleans area students may have lost in the storm. A family benefit night was held at a restaurant that was one of our business partners, and with the proceeds, we purchased two digital cameras, printers, and art supplies for our "adopted' school. In late November, the art teacher and her husband drove to the town and personally delivered all the items to the school. Our students continued to create ceramic pins and magnets for each holiday, and the art club continued its sales. The most popular were the hearts made and sold during the week of Valentine's Day. One of our partners, the city's medical center, even sold the hearts in their gift shop! In the spring, our student art club sent the principal of our partner school a check for over $2,000 as a result of the efforts of our students and community.

- **Our adopted partner school in Louisiana** was so thankful for our community's efforts to help their community and their children they wrote us a letter at the end of their school year and promised us they would do as we did for them—work hard and be kind. One year after the hurricane, the principal of our adopted school decided to surprise our art teacher and came to personally say thank you. You see, they were childhood friends and grew up together in that town outside of New Orleans. We pulled off the surprise in front of our whole student body. That principal brought tears to everyone's eyes and joy to everyone's hearts when she gave us a framed, handmade, New Orleans quilt, an inscription on a plaque, and a framed picture of her and her happy students with their letter of appreciation. Their school was much like ours—an inclusive environment with special-needs students who cared so much for their community. We had made friends for life!

Democracy: The American Dream

During my last year at my school, we decided it was time for an important conversation we needed to have in our learning organization. What exactly was the "American Dream," and what did it mean to us? Was it owning a house and having a job and family? Was it life, liberty, and the pursuit of happiness? Was it a free and appropriate education for all students? For me, it was certainly creating a safe and innovative learning environment for all students, parents, teachers, staff, and our community. It was about everyone feeling valued, important, and included and believing they could grow and become. It was celebrating successes and setting the tone and high expectations at the beginning of and throughout every school year. It was building relationships and creating a community family who cared about each other, listened to each other, and offered kindness and love. It was designing and creating quality work that authentically engaged students in the learning process. It was making connections for students and ourselves so we could think both critically and creatively. It was creating the WOW School of the Century! It was giving all students a quality, *public* education and bringing back the joy and love of learning. Doesn't every child in America deserve this?

Relationships

"The greatest compliment that was ever paid to me was when someone asked me what I thought and attended to my answer."
—Henry David Thoreau

How to Rally Communities to Save Public Schools

Imagine you wake up tomorrow and read in the headlines of your local paper, "Communities Rally to Save Public Schools!" How would you react? Would you say, "It will never work," "It's about time," or "Finally. I've been a part of something that's making a difference"? Do you believe we can do this? Will you join me?

Creating a Movement

"A movement is a group of people with a shared purpose who create change together. It is made up of a strong pipeline of leaders, powerful grassroots support, solid partnerships and a shared political goal and plan for the future. Movements can change the world by getting laws passed and enforced, advancing social, political and economic justice for marginalized groups, and changing culture and how people behave. A combination of strategies are used: advocacy, media reach, legal action, protests and research" (www.globalfundforwomen.org).

- **Can we create a movement to reprioritize public education?** I believe we can! Most of us are guilty of accepting the status quo or the wrath that reigns down on us from the "powers that be." Why?

Maybe it is because we are only one little person and we can't change the world by ourselves. Maybe it is because we do not have the time, energy, or persistence to get involved for the long-term because we have jobs, families, and lots of other responsibilities. Maybe we fear the consequences of speaking or acting in opposition to those in power. Remember, we live in a democracy, and each of us has a voice. Let me share an example of the power of one.

- **The Trimtab Factor** was first used by brilliant inventor, architect, and philosopher Buckminster Fuller. He served on a naval ship during World War I and used the metaphor of the trim tab to show what just one person can do. Picture a large oceangoing ship traveling at a high speed through the water. The mass and momentum of the vessel are enormous, and great force is needed to turn the ship's rudder and change its direction. Attached to the rudder is a tiny little mechanism called the trim tab. By turning the trim tab, one person can exert a small amount of pressure and turn the enormous ship. Thus, the Trimtab Factor shows how the precise application of a small amount of leverage can produce a powerful effect! Imagine what could happen if each of us became a trim tab leader and an agent for change.

Partnerships

I've talked at great length about the importance of building relationships and how those relationships can become partnerships to enhance and improve the quality of public education. So how do we get started?

- **School leadership can initiate partnerships with parents and families** by reaching out and inviting them to school to meet and share ideas about what they would like to see happen with the education of their children. You should allow time for them to also share their concerns, not about their individual child, but about the school and policies in general. A private appointment can be set up to discuss specific, individual concerns. Remember to listen with empathy and understanding and put yourself in their shoes. Listen to their voice, look into their eyes, watch their body language, and let them know you care. Phone calls or face-to-face contact is best, but a written invitation can also be effective.

- **School leadership can initiate partnerships with businesses and communities** by reaching out and extending an invitation to them to attend events at your school. Again, stopping by their business and inviting them face-to-face is the most effective way, though phone calls and written invitations can also work. A School Advisory Council meeting would show them how you are open to input from the community and how transparent you are with sharing budgetary and operational challenges. An event that includes student performances with teacher direction demonstrates the creativity and innovation at your school, and they will want to come back for more!

- **Businesses can also initiate partnerships with schools.** If you have a small business and want to make contacts in the community, think of what you may be able to offer your neighborhood school. It is not about making sales but about volunteering and building relationships that will reward your business many times over for any time and expertise you choose to share. If you work for a larger company that allows time off to volunteer in the community, stop by your local school. You will need to go through the volunteer application process, but in no time you will be contributing to the success of our future workers and leaders.

- **Businesses can recruit other businesses through their local chamber of commerce organizations.** Connections made between businesses happen all the time at local chamber breakfasts. As a business, share the positive experiences you've had with your neighborhood school with others. As a chamber, invite local school leaders to your breakfasts, and make connections with them and their schools, as they are educational business leaders too.

Government

- **Local governments can communicate with schools and businesses to increase public-school desirability and change public perception about schools.** My school's local government invited school leaders to a monthly luncheon at city hall to share the services their departments could bring to our schools and to listen to school leaders about their school's needs.

- **School leaders can invite government leaders to their schools** to share lessons about government and being a good citizen. Our government leaders were always happy to speak and attend our school community events, as they got to meet and hear from their constituents. There should never be political agendas or solicitations at these venues.

Nonprofit Organizations

Working with children, families, and communities to improve quality of life is the goal of most nonprofit organizations. Their role is to raise funds from major corporations and benefactors and to connect these donors with those in need. Nonprofits can also inform their funding base of the needs of public schools and their communities.

- **Education foundations in the state of Florida** were formed by local school districts after legislation was passed in 1984, allowing them to raise private funds to support public school students, teachers, and schools. In 1987, the Consortium of Florida Education Foundations (CFEF) was created to provide support at local levels. Florida funding allows a dollar-for-dollar match to local foundations for charitable giving that supports student achievement.

- **As a retired principal, I volunteer** for my local education foundation by serving on the Community Engagement Committee and facilitating community conversations about public education. Training is provided by the CFEF, and we use a Harwood

Institute strategic process called "Turning Outward." This process turns the focus from the internal system to the community's aspirations and challenges and how they can specifically help their students and local schools. Instead of another talking head from a school district, this process engages the community by first defining what a perfect school or system looks like (aspirations) and then defining the problem as it exists (challenges). Additional, probing questions are asked, ideas are charted and shared, and a list of possible solutions is prioritized. Follow-up is key to the success of this process. One example of this process, which I facilitated, was a meeting with teachers at a break-out session of the Education Foundation's Innovative Teacher Grant Conference. The Partners in Education Board of business leaders was about to come under the umbrella of the foundation's community-involvement arm. Teachers had already targeted a lack of resources as a challenge they faced with business partners in their schools—not monetary resources but human resources that would allow students to be paired with mentors and role models, as well as exposing their students to a variety of career options for their futures. The career options suggested were not only college-ready careers but also agriculture and trade careers. Their overarching aspiration was to prepare students for the world of work. An exciting outcome from that organizational merger was a business leader stepping up to provide a pilot program for high school students so that they would be prepared with the "soft skills" they need to write a résumé, interview, and dress for success on the job. This impressive foundation has funded educational programs for schools, given $2.6 million in teacher-innovation grants, and donated $12 million in materials and supplies and $11 million in scholarships for students.

Several teachers at our school were pros at writing innovation grants for their classrooms, and one year they wrote and received a $10,000 superintendent's grant for a school-wide innovation in technology!

No Additional Tax Dollars

- **Organizing communities and meeting together as an informed, focused group does not cost any additional taxpayer dollars!** Using schools or public facilities to meet is cost neutral. Inviting others in the spirit of volunteerism to do whatever it takes to reclaim our schools is cost neutral. Proposing cost-neutral solutions to local school boards, state and federal legislators, and community business and organization leaders will certainly get their attention!

- **Creating volunteer work groups to research and contact those currently in decision-making power does not cost additional taxpayer dollars.** Arrange to meet with elected officials at the local, state, and national levels to suggest workable solutions. Coordinate a trip to your state legislature to speak on behalf of your public-school communities. Be sure to include your PTA and school advisory groups who have more power, as parents, to affect change than educator-only groups. Present a united front in advocating change for the best interests of children, and offer solutions and ideas of how to work together to make that happen.

Our Future: Our Children and Our Democracy

- **Our children are the future of our country, our society, and of humanity.** Is it too much to ask for each person reading this to write down at least one way they can contribute to the success of our future leaders and caretakers? What can you do as a teacher, parent, business, or community member to save our public schools for the greater good of our country's welfare? Do you have a friend you can ask to join you in this quest? What specific expertise do you have to move this process forward? Is it making phone calls or organizing meetings with government and legislative leaders? Can you speak about the current reality of our public education system with a local group you belong to?

- **The loss of historical events** is happening right before our very eyes! Statues are being removed, and streets are being renamed to defy the glorification of historical figures who were anti civil rights, but what if these facts are also erased from our history as a nation? Is it possible that if we don't remember the lessons we've learned, we will make the same mistakes?

- **What do we want our future to look like?** Imagine a world where schools are separated by the belief systems of families or collectives whose children attend their neighborhood schools. The students are taught only about what the group believes and wants them to know. There may be no science, history, or creative arts, and no children who come from foreign countries and speak languages other than English. The curriculum is regulated by a process that allows anyone in the collective community to remove anything objectionable to their beliefs. Each school is operated by a for-profit corporation whose success is measured by students who are allowed to repeat only the information they are fed. If the child does not comply with the corporation and cannot be successfully remediated, they are removed from the school. Most teachers have left their schools because they failed to meet the elusive evaluation formulas created by the government and enforced by the corporation. No one is allowed to speak on subjects about the world beyond their community, such as the effects of climate change or the Founding Fathers of the Constitution and our democracy. Future generations will never know these things existed. Conversation and individual thinking are prohibited! Is this Orwell's *1984*, a Star Trek movie, or the current reality of public schools?

    "But public schools have a belief system too," you may respond. Yes, they do, but that belief system supports life, liberty, and the pursuit of happiness, as well as equal opportunity and a free and appropriate education for all. I believe I'll stick with the beliefs supported in our United States Constitution and our democratic process. But what about a situation in the news where a teacher has bullied a student or chosen to teach topics specific to a religious belief or an antidemocratic process restricted by public educational law? The teacher choosing to teach restricted content is writing their own "pink slip" and should go to a private or parochial school where those topics are allowed. And the teacher who bullies a student does not belong in any educational classroom with children!

- **Current Reality #1** is frightfully closing in on the scenario I have painted. On July 1, 2017, a new Florida law (CS/HB 989) took effect, allowing a parent or any county resident to object to the use of a specific instructional material and present evidence to require a school board to discontinue use of that material. This law was not passed with the parent in mind, because processes already exist where parents can object to instructional materials at the local level. This law was passed to support the political agendas of government officials and the corporate interests that pad their pockets. The fear here reflects the total denial of the scientific theory of climate change and the removal of that free idea from the government vocabulary. The fact is, in 2015, Florida's governor Rick Scott ordered the State Department of Environmental Protection not to use the words "climate change," "global warming," or "sustainability" in any reports or other official communications. Another fear is the removal of historical atrocities such as the Holocaust or slavery. Public education allows the discussion and debate of different ideas and sides of an issue and freedom for students to theorize, think both critically and creatively, and make individual and personal decisions. You may not agree, but remember, public schools were designed to support the common good of all people.

- **Current Reality #2** is the new Florida law (CS/HB 7069) I outlined in the last chapter. It includes an appropriation of $413,950,000 in recurring general revenue funds to establish "Schools of Hope" and "hope providers" for parents of students in low-performing schools so they have a choice of another high-quality school option. The fear is that this law makes it easier for privately managed or for-profit charter schools to receive this public-school, tax-payer funding to boost the operation of their schools. Again, charter schools in Florida are unregulated and do not have to hire certified teachers or admit students with special needs.

- **Current Reality #3** is the same Florida law (CS/HB 7069), which spends $214 million (a 400 percent increase) on the "Best and Brightest" Bonus Program for teachers, which is largely based on the teachers' standardized test scores from *high school*, along with evaluation instruments invented by companies related to or who give large donations to politicians' campaigns. This 214-page bill, by the way, was tied to the state budget and was crafted and voted on behind closed doors in the eleventh hour and not with the transparency called for by Florida's Sunshine Law! I am not against providing additional school-choice options for parents and their children. What I am against is an elite group of big businesses and wealthy politicians deciding the fate of our children and the future of America.

What is the current reality in your world? Will you make a commitment to stop the momentum of this wave of privatization at the state and national levels to replace the idea and reality of public schools?

I know there are thousands of innovative and customer-focused public schools across our great nation. I see them in my own backyard as technology entrepreneurs coding and designing video games and computer apps, and exploring engineering and robotics. I watch them using critical thinking skills to strategize a chess game in a school tournament. I hear them presenting a persuasive argument in a debate on a controversial topic, wearing a business suit and looking like the next Clarence Darrow. I believe we, as learning organizations, can transform our public schools so that all children receive the quality education they deserve. I also believe that we, as learning communities and in the name of democracy and freedom, can take back our public schools from greedy decision makers.

I believe there is hope for our future and the future of quality public education for all!

Relationships

"You don't develop courage by being happy in your relationships every day. You develop it by surviving difficult times and challenging adversity."
—*Epicurus*

The Dream Continues

Thank you for joining me in my personal quest for quality public education. I am a practitioner. The ideas and thoughts I've shared are not a magic formula I've made up. They are a composite of my learning from the best educational leaders, whom I've read, studied, and had the pleasure to meet or work with over the years. I hope you've learned from my struggles and joys and felt my passion for the work. Phil Schlechty used to say "Real work is real hard." Heaven knows it is not easy work, but it is rewarding work. You can see it in the eyes of all children who believe in themselves.

I did not tell you about the three years I left my school and went to work at the district level. It was a year after I was awarded the honor of National Distinguished Principal. I thought I was *expected* to climb the ladder and make a bigger impact, but I was wrong.

And that is a story for another time . . . and another book.

References and Resources

Chapter 1

Covey, Stephen R. *The 7 Habits of Highly Effective People: Powerful Lessons in Personal Change.* New York, NY: Simon & Schuster, 1989.

Angelou, Maya http://www.goodreads.com/quotes

Howard, Joseph, *Sister Act.* Directed by Emile Ardolino. Touchstone Pictures, 1992.

Disney Institute. *Four Keys of Customer Service.* "Marketing Your School Training," 1992.

Buckingham, Marcus, and Donald O. Clifton. *Soar with Your Strengths.* New York, NY: Delacorte Press, 1992.

Chapter 2

Blanchard, Ken, and Sheldon Bowles. *High Five! The Magic of Working Together.* New York, NY: William Morrow, 2000.

Chapter 3

Sparks, Denis. "The Educator Examined: An Interview with Phillip Schlechty, 10 Critical Qualities of Student Work," *Journal of Staff Development* (summer 1998).

Peters, Tom. *The Pursuit of Wow: Every Person's Guide to Topsy-Turvy Times.* New York, NY: Vintage Books, 1994.

Sizer, Ted. *Horace's Compromise.* New York, NY: Houghton/Mifflin, 1984; Sizer is also the founder of the Coalition of Essential Schools and Ten Common Principles. See http://www.essentialschools.org.

Yarrow, Peter. Of Peter, Paul and Mary, and founder of Operation Respect (2000). *Don't Laugh at Me,* music by Allen Shamblin and Steve Seskin, lyrics by Mark Willis. http://www.operationrespect.org/.

Carbo, Marie. *Teaching Students to Read Through Their Individual Learning Styles.* New York, NY: Pearson, 1987; Carbo is the founder of the National Reading Styles Institute. http://www.nrsi.com.

Grant, Jim, and Bob Johnson. *A Common-Sense Guide to Multiage Practices*, Boston: Teachers Pub. Group, 1994. Bob Johnson is the founder of Staff Development for Educators (SDE).

Canady, Robert. "A Cure for Fragmented Schedules in Elementary Schools." *Educational Leadership* (October 1988). http://www.schoolschedulingassociates.com/.

Schlechty, Phillip C. "On Restructuring Roles and Relationships: A Conversation with Phil Schlechty." Interview by Ron Brandt. *Educational Leadership Journal of Association of Curriculum and Development* (ASCD), 1993.

Images of School http://www.schlechtycenter.org/tools

I Love Lucy and the Chocolate Factory. Youtube.com/watch?v=WmAwcMNxGqM.

Chapter 4

Fullan, Michael. "Change Theory: A Force for School Improvement." Center for Strategic Education (CSE). Paper no. 157, November 2006.

Disney Institute. *Navigating Change.* "Marketing Your School Training," 1992.

Barker, Joel. *Paradigm Pioneers. Discovering the Future* Series, Burnsville, MN: Charthouse International Learning Corporation, Starthrower Distribution, 1993. Video.

Schlechty, Dr. Phillip C. "On the Frontier of School Reform with Trailblazers, Pioneers, and Settlers." *Journal of Staff Development.* ASCD, Fall 1993.

Blanchard, Ken and Don Shula. *Everyone's a Coach: Five Business Secrets for High-Performance Coaching.* Nashville, TN: Zondervan, 1996.

Blanchard, Ken, and Sheldon Bowels. *Raving Fans: A Revolutionary Approach to Customer Service.* New York, NY: William Morrow, 1993.

Rodenberry, Gene. *Star Trek* (1966–69). "To boldly go where no one has gone before." Culver, CA: Backlot Desilu Studios (1966) and Hollywood, CA: Paramount Studios (1967–69).

Wheatley, Margaret J. *Leadership and the New Science: Learning About Organization from an Orderly Universe.* Oakland, CA: Berrett-Koehler Publishers, 1996.

Ritz Carlton/about/gold standards motto: "We are Ladies and Gentlemen serving Ladies and Gentlemen." http://www.ritzcarlton.com.

Jet Blue/corporate social responsibility/mission: "To inspire humanity both in the air and on the ground." http://www.jetblue.com.

Nordstrom/about us/customer service: "To provide outstanding service every day, one customer at a time; empowering employees to use their best judgment." http://www.nordstrom.com.

Schlechty, Phillip. *Working on the Work Design Qualities.* http://www.schlechtycenter.org/tools.

Chapter 5

Singleton, Glenn E., and Curtis Linton. *Courageous Conversations About Race: A Field Guide for Achieving Equity in Schools.* Thousand Oaks, CA: Corwin Press, 2005.

Schlechty, Phillip. *Shaking Up the Schoolhouse: How to Support and Sustain Educational Innovation.* New York, NY: Jossey-Bass Publishers, 2000.

Chapter 6

Marzano, Robert. www.learningsciences.com/wp/wp-content/uploads/2017/06/Focus-Eval-Model-Overview-20170321.pdf

Strauss, Valerie. Here's What Jeb Bush Really Did to Public Education in Florida. Washington, D. C.: *The Washington Post*, June 15, 2015.

Ravitch, Diane. *Reign of Error: The Hoax of the Privatization Movement and the Danger to America's Public Schools.* New York, NY: Vintage Books, 2014.

Dunn, Tracy, Loeffelholz, and Pibel. *Why Corporations Want Our Public Schools.* Bainbridge Island, WA, Education Uprising Edition. *Yes! Magazine* (spring 2014).

Schlechty, Phillip. *Shaking Up the Schoolhouse: How to Support and Sustain Educational Innovation.* New York, NY: Jossey-Bass Publishers, 2000.

Christiansen, Clayton M. *The Innovator's Dilemma: When Technologies Cause Great Firms to Fail.* Boston, MA: Harvard Business School Press, 2016.

Schlechty, Phillip C. *Creating Great Schools: Six Critical Systems at the Heart of Educational Innovation.* New York, NY: Jossey-Bass Publishers, 2005.

Chapter 7

Johnson, Spencer, M.D. *Who Moved My Cheese: An Amazing Way to Deal with Change in Your Work and in Your Life.* New York, NY: J. P. Putnam's Sons, 1998.

Blanchard, Ken, and Sheldon Bowles. *High Five! The Magic of Working Together.* New York, NY: William Morrow, 2000.

Keene, Ellin Oliver, and Susan Zimmerman. *Mosaic of Thought: Teaching Comprehension in a Reader's Workshop.* New York, NY: Heineman, 1997.

South Florida Center for Educational Leaders, Barry University School of Education. Gayle Moller, Executive Director. Affiliation with International Network of Principals Centers, Harvard Graduate School of Education.

Colick, Lewis, Joe Johnson, Charles Gordon, and Larry Franco. *October Sky.* Writer: Lewis Colick, Directed by Joe Johnson. Universal Pictures, 2005. Based on the memoir *Rocket Boys* by Homer Hickam.

Zemeckis, Robert. *The Polar Express.* Directed by Robert Zemeckis. Warner Brothers, 2005. Based on the book, *The Polar Express*, by Chris Van Allsburg, New York, NY: HMH Books for Young Readers, 2005.

Chapter 8

National Science Foundation, (1998). STEM (Science, Technology, Engineering, and Mathematics), developed in accordance with the American Competitiveness and Workforce Improvement Act of 1998. http://www.nsf.gov.

Principal PROMiSE Program, (2008). Partnership to Rejuvenate and Optimize Mathematics and Science Education in Florida. U.S. Department of Education, Florida Department of Education and Florida State University.

STEM + Art = STEAM. http://www.stemtosteam.org.

Obama, Michelle. "Let's Move," 2009. http://www.letsmove.obamawhitehouse.archives.gov.

Jump Rope for Heart, (1979). American Heart Association. http://www.heart.org/HEARTORG.

Renzulli, Joseph and Sally Reis. Renzulli School-Wide Enrichment Model (SEM), 1985. University of Connecticut, Center for Creativity, Gifted Education and Talent Development. http://www.renzullilearning.com.

Chapter 9

Thomas Jefferson to Joseph C. Cabell. *On Politics and Government.* "Educate Every Citizen," Monticello Jan. 14, 1818.

The Horace Mann League of the USA. http://www.hmleague.org/.

Roosevelt, Franklin D. Message for American Education Week, 1938. http://www.presidency.ucsb.edu.

PL 94-142, (1975) reauthorized as Individuals with Disabilities Act (IDEA) in 2004, amended in 2015 as PL-114-95, Every Student Succeeds Act.

Coalition of Adult Basic Education http://www.coabe.org.

Junior Achievement http://www.juniorachievement.org.

Chapter 10

Creating a Movement. http://www.globalfundforwomen.org.

Fuller, Buckminster. "The Trimtab Factor." Interview with Rob Sayre. *Playboy* (2009). Character, (1972). Excellence and Process Blog, http://www.characterandexcellence.wordpress.com.

Consortium of Florida Education Foundations (CFEF) http://www.educationfoundationsfl.org.

Broward Education Foundation (BEF) http://www.browardeducationfoundation.org.

Harwood Institute for Public Innovation. http://www.theharwoodinstitute.org and youtube.com/user/HarwoodInstitute.

Orwell, George. *1984.* New York, NY: Signet Classics,1961.

Note to the Reader

Thank you so much for taking the time to read my book. I hope you've found inspiration within for your own support of quality public education. If you found the message useful, it would mean a great deal to me if you could leave me a review on Amazon and Goodreads—and, of course, spread the word!

With deepest gratitude,

Susan

About the Author

Susan A. Colton is a retired elementary school principal who spent twenty-two years in school administration with Broward County Public Schools, Florida, the sixth largest school system in the nation. She served as principal of two elementary schools and director of leadership development at the district office. Susan has more than thirty years of educational experience, also as a classroom teacher and an educational consultant with Macmillan Publishing Company. She had wanted to be a teacher since she was six-years old and an only child who loved to teach (and boss) her teddy bears and dolls.

As a school principal, she held several leadership roles, including chairperson of her elementary school principals' organization, where she served with the leadership of more than 130 public elementary schools. She was also a member of the Superintendent's Leadership Team at the time. Susan served as lead principal for both feeder patterns of schools, or innovation zones, during her principalships and was a member of the groundbreaking district committee that established Character Education and the eight core character traits: *Responsibility, Citizenship, Kindness, Respect, Honesty, Self-Control, Tolerance,* and *Cooperation.* In 1999, she received the Florida Commissioner's Award for Outstanding Leadership, and in 2000 was named a National Distinguished Principal, representing public school leadership on behalf of the state of Florida at our nation's capital. In 2013, Susan was selected as one of seven inaugural Hall of Fame Distinguished Alumni by the Broward Education Foundation and received her very own granite star in the Walk of Fame outside district headquarters.

For fun, Susan was an "awesome alto" with the Singing Principals, performing at major local events and national principal conferences, and acclaimed "Goodwill Ambassadors" for Broward County. For the fortieth anniversary of the organization, the Singing Principals performed a stand-alone concert at the Broward Center for the Performing Arts in downtown Fort Lauderdale. Although she loved performing, Susan's favorite part of being with the Singing Principals was the camaraderie she experienced at the after-school rehearsals held at one of the local elementary schools.

In 2013, Susan retired to care for her mother, who had Parkinson's disease. In 2016, she lost not only her mother (in February) but also her best friend (in October), as well as her husband (right before Christmas). This past year, she has worked on reinventing herself and rediscovering who she is. She volunteers with the Broward Education Foundation, serving on the Community Engagement Committee and facilitating community conversations about public education.

Susan lives in Pompano Beach, Florida, with her two cats, Miss Kitty and Mr. Bojangles.

www.ingramcontent.com/pod-product-compliance
Lightning Source LLC
Chambersburg PA
CBHW070738020526
44118CB00035B/1500